TWELVE STRANDS

TWELVE STRANDS

Journeys with Asian Authors

Edited by Bernice Lee

GRACEW♥RKS

Published by Graceworks Pte Ltd
22 Sin Ming Lane
#04-76 Midview City
Singapore 573969
Email: enquiries@graceworks.com.sg
Website: www.graceworks.com.sg

Scripture quotations are taken from The Holy Bible, English
Standard Version®. Copyright © 2001 by Crossway Bibles, a
division of Good News Publishers. All rights reserved.

A CIP record for this book is available from the National
Library Board, Singapore.

Design by Intent Design and Consultancy Pte Ltd

ISBN: 978-981-09-6606-5

2 3 4 5 6 7 8 9 10 . 24 23 22 21 20 19

CONTENTS

PREFACE

It was more than 20 years ago that the first collection of author journeys was commissioned by Media Associates International (MAI) in Latin America. Shortly after, African and Asian compilations were also published. The latter, *An Asian Palette* (Singapore: Armour Publishing, 1998), has inspired many budding writers in their journeys. The heartfelt stories in that volume also encouraged many who were struggling in their craft. Knowing that one is not alone in the solitary journey of writing is often part of the battle won.

Since then, both MAI-Asia and MAI-Africa have come into being, to consolidate and grow the work of MAI in Asia and Africa, respectively. In this tenth year of MAI-Asia's existence, we thought it timely to hear from a fresh set of voices, some of whom have actually benefited from the combined wisdom captured in the first Asian volume.

Twelve Strands, as the name suggests, pulls together the writing journeys of 12 Asian authors from countries as diverse as South Korea and Pakistan. Some write poetry and songs, while others write children's books. Some are able to share the deepest pains and highest joys of those whose testimonies they give voice to. All feel an almost compulsive need to write so that the knowledge of the love of Christ can reach the farthest corners of their country, if not the world. They share a calling.

In recounting her journey after finding herself voiceless because of a rare disease, Emily Lim said that "Like Dorothy and her friends, the Cowardly Lion, the Scarecrow and the Tin Man, in L. Frank Baum's *The Wizard of Oz*, my journey similarly took me in search of voice, courage, clarity of thought and a new heart. It led me on a deeper search for meaning in life and discovery of a new and different kind of voice. A voice that emerged from the written word."

Abu Taher Chowdhury was one of those you would call an unlikely writer. His great desire to save the lost impelled him to find a way to reach them and, when he saw the life-transforming impact of a tract, he knew this was the way to go: "I didn't know the ABCs of writing. Basically, I was not a bright student, and it was difficult for me to even spell more difficult words. I could not speak well as I had problems with proper pronunciation. But that booklet gave me new courage through its simple unspoken message— 'Books can change lives.'"

Andrew Yuan, who grappled with the irony of writing books about marriage even as his own was foundering learnt precious lessons from God during the process. In the end, he concluded that "Writing is like having a fishbone in your throat. You have to get it out."

This book in your hand is our small offering to those who have fishbones that need to come out. May you be inspired to hone your craft so that:

> Posterity will serve him;
> future generations will be told about the Lord.
> They will proclaim his righteousness,
> declaring to a people yet unborn:
> He has done it!
>
> *Psalm 22:30, 31*

BERNICE LEE
November 2015

MY LEGACY OF WRITING

TINA CHO is the author of *The Girl's Guide to Manners* (Legacy Press Kids, 2014) and a coloring book, *God Is So Good* (Warner Press, 2013). *Seasons of the Asian Pear Tree* is forthcoming from Schoolwide along with two nonfiction books from Legacy Press Kids, and *Korean Celebrations* from Tuttle. Tina writes for the educational and children's markets from South Korea. She is a wife, mom to two kids, and a 1st grade teacher. You can find Tina at her blog, tinamcho.com.

How It All Started

The summer of 2008, my career changed course. Previously, I had taught elementary grades for 11 years in the United States. My husband, two kids, and I had moved from Arizona to California, but for the first time, I was unable to get a teaching job. The economy wasn't doing well, and I didn't have any contacts in these school districts. Painfully, I told God if He didn't want me to teach anymore, I would obey Him. It was when I surrendered to God's leading that He led me into another dream of mine — writing for children.

I had wanted to leave a Christian legacy for my own children. And since I had loved children's picture books from my days of teaching, I decided to learn how to write them. I searched the Internet and found an organization, the Society of Children's Book Writers and Illustrators (SCBWI). They gave me the name of a lady who headed up children's writing critique groups in my area. I discovered she was a Christian writer of over 75 books. I couldn't believe how God was leading! She invited me to her writing group that met once a month. I was so nervous yet excited to meet them. Before my first meeting, I told God, "If this is what you might have for me, then please let them like my story." After reading them my very first manuscript, they said they couldn't believe I had just started writing. They thought I was joking. Unbelievable! Me — a writer? I hated writing papers in college.

This Christian author, Nancy I. Sanders, took me under her wing. I studied all about writing and was in her local writing group and her online picture book critique group, Pens and Brushes, which had seven other members from around the nation.

First Sale

The wonderful ladies in my local group encouraged me to submit a story to a private Christian school's developing reading program. Some of the others in my group were part of the cadre of freelance writers. So I prepared a story according to a set theme and submitted it. About three weeks later, I received a cheque in the mail. I remember my husband bounding down the stairs as I showed it to him. He was amazed that I had received money for something I had written. That acceptance began a string of acceptances with the Christian school's reading program. It was great practice for what God had in store later.

Write What You Know

As I studied the craft of writing, I read many books, such as *Yes! You Can Learn How to Write Children's Books, Get Them Published, and Build a Successful Writing Career* by Nancy Sanders. I read writing blogs and freelance writing sites to find my niche. Nancy taught me how to query publishers with ideas before writing the manuscript.

Once I found interesting publishers to query, I studied their publications or websites and then emailed them a list of ideas. One of the places I sent a query to was an e-zine called *Grands,* an online magazine for grandparents. The ironic thing is that I wasn't even a grandparent. I was a mother of two kids, aged six and three! But I sent them a query anyway, and the editor emailed that she wanted a story about a family with a set of close grandparents and a set of long-distance grandparents and how they kept the balance. I emailed the editor back and told her that in our case both sets of grandparents were long-distance, one set in Iowa, and the

> ... it's amazing how God prepares us little by little, step by step, for the tasks He entrusts to us.

other in South Korea. Well, she came up with the idea of me writing an article on how my kids kept up a relationship with their overseas grandparents in Korea. This led to a contract sale! The editor was great to work with and helped me hone my writing skills. I even supplied them with photographs of my kids and my in-laws, plus a Korean recipe. Better yet, they sent a photographer to my house to do a photo shoot with my kids! It was so much fun. My kids ended up on the cover of the e-zine! I felt like a real writer. That article was published in July 2009.

I think it's amazing how God prepares us little by little, step by step, for the tasks He entrusts to us. One evening my husband brought home a free hamster, cage and all, from a coworker. We knew nothing about taking care of hamsters. During this time, God had led me to start writing book reviews for the *Christian Library Journal* (CLJ). I received free books, and all I had to do was write the reviews and submit them to the editor. God has a sense of humor. My first assignment for them was to review books about small pets, such as *Caring for Your Hamster* and *Hamsters and Gerbils*. So that's why we had a hamster! For the next year I continued writing book reviews.

Aside from writing for the Christian school's reading program and book reviews for CLJ, my first children's story published was a rebus (a story with some pictures that stand for words) for the now defunct children's e-zine *Stories for Children*. My mentor, Nancy Sanders, encouraged us to also write for the low-pay/no-pay markets like *Stories for Children,* because they are hungry for submissions and will also take first-time writers, like myself. My husband and I had taken our kids miniature golfing, and that led to another story idea. I turned our outing into a rebus story that sold as "Golf Ball Mystery." That rebus started my joy of writing more rebuses.

My writing friends told me about Focus on the Family's Christian magazine for children called *Clubhouse Jr.* My first story to them was rejected. Then I sent them a rebus about another place my kids loved to go to — the beach. It sold. Since then I've had three other rebus stories published by them. The stars of these stories are my children because I use their names and experiences. It's always a thrill for them to see their names in print.

Having a good relationship with the *Clubhouse Jr* editor has helped me sell two nonfiction animal articles to them too. It's fun to write these with a Christian perspective and include a Bible verse. The magazine also has a Bible story each month. I wanted to give this a try as well. So I prayed for God to give me a story idea. One morning as I read my daily devotions, 1 Chronicles 25 jumped out at me. "This would be great as a retold Bible story for Father's Day," I said to myself. So I wrote the story, had a friend critique it, and then submitted it to my editor. It sold. I pray that these stories will speak to children's hearts as I continue to write for this publication.

Educational Writing

As a former teacher, God used my career of teaching for educational writing. And this has become one of my niches. I discovered the website Education.com and saw that they needed crafts and educational activities for children. I studied what they already had and then wrote a query offering other ideas. I sold over 25 activities to them. My kids had fun helping me develop the crafts. My kitchen was turned into lab of sorts where we tested ideas and took photographs. The editor even asked me to develop a special series of activities/crafts for that May's Asian American month! Little did I know God was preparing me for an even bigger task in the years to come!

I was very excited to write this book and was on the edge of my seat waiting for her call.

During this time in California, God spoke to me to spend more time with Him. I was inspired by my mentor Nancy again, as she always spent one hour with God each morning. So I decided to give it a try. Sure, it was hard to pull myself out of bed and stay alert during that hour. But I prayed, read the Bible, and listened to sermons online. And you know what? God blessed! I saw an ad in our newspaper for an educational writer for Lakeshore Learning not too far from where I lived. I knew of this place because as a teacher we dreamed of buying their products for our classrooms. So I applied, took a writing test, and was called in to a meeting full of writers, editors, and product developers. Whoa! I was very intimidated as this was my first big writing job. I was still a newbie. We sat around the table as the product developer described what she wanted this educational project to look like. I was thrilled just to be in the building, let alone chosen to write on the project. Writing these phonic guided reading books was right up my alley. I loved every minute of it. And this assignment led to writing for them on and off for the next several years. God was using my teaching experience once again.

Down in the Dumps

I also learned how to write book proposals during this time. Again, I queried an editor regarding a nonfiction idea, and she said to write a proposal. I had no idea how, and so my super mentor, Nancy, filled me in on all the details. I spent almost two months researching and writing the proposal. The editor took my proposal to her editorial meeting. I was very excited to write this book and was on the edge of my seat waiting for her call. Well, the call didn't turn out like I expected. Someone else had written a proposal on the same idea, and her proposal had won. I was very disappointed. I think I even cried. I had spent all that time researching, reading thick, dusty books from the library. But then I read a verse in the Bible, Psalm 118:22. "The stone the builders rejected has become the capstone; the Lord has done this, and it is marvelous in our eyes." This verse spoke to me. Jesus had been rejected, yet it was turned into a marvelous thing. And God exalted Him. Sure, my rejection hurt, especially this one, but after thinking how Jesus had been rejected, I somehow felt better. God can work through even my rejections. I had learnt the lesson from my past experiences that God would have something better planned. I was sure my book proposal writing skill would not be wasted.

A Change

Rejections aside, my writing life was going great. I'd drop my daughter off at school, and then I'd work on writing activities the rest of the day and also play with my son. All that changed in 2010, though, when my husband announced that he wanted to move back to South Korea. I was devastated to say the least. I'd have to give up my writing group, Nancy, my friends, family, and American culture. Eventually, through lots of prayer, God gave me peace about the move. And He didn't forget my writing. More on that later.

> One of the reasons I wanted to write was to leave a legacy for my children.

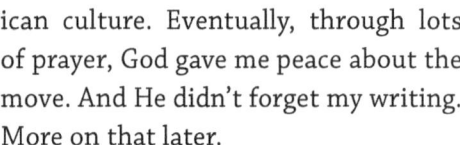

Even though I felt like a lone writer, I still had my online picture book critique group. They have been such a wonderful source of encouragement to me; and many in my face-to-face group also continued to email. God soon showed me He could use my writing abilities even though I was across the ocean. Back in 2009 I had sent some book ideas to a Christian publisher in San Diego. In 2011 the editor emailed to send a proposal!

A New Legacy

I used what I had previously learned with book proposals and took another month to research and write this new idea. One of the reasons I wanted to write was to leave a legacy for my children. And this book was one of the ways I could do it. The proposal was accepted by the publisher, whose name, would you believe, had "legacy" in its title. I wrote the book. *The Girls' Guide to Manners and All That Great Stuff* will be coming out soon! And it will be perfect for my daughter.

Once again, this relationship with the editor has led to two more books. I was invited to write book proposals for two in-house ideas. *My Mini Pet Shop* and *The Girls' Guide to Going Green* will also be published soon. I pray girls will enjoy these books and have fun reading the stories and doing the devotions, crafts, activities, and puzzles. Do you see how God used my previous craft and activity writing along with proposal writing?

A Surprise

God had something else for me…I received an email from an editor I had written to two years earlier regarding ideas for a coloring book. I had totally forgotten that I had emailed her. I don't draw, but this Christian publisher accepted manuscripts for the words in a coloring book. I had been inspired by my then three-year-old son. How could I explain to him that God is good? Back when we were living in California, I had taken the words to the popular chorus, "God is so good," and written ways that little kids could see God's goodness in their lives. The editor said she had saved my manuscript and wanted to know if it was still available. My goodness, YES! So in 2013 my coloring book *God Is So Good* was published by Warner Press.

Another way God used my educational writing was in the writing of activities for Focus on the Family's *Thriving Family* magazine and lesson plans for another educational publisher, Gryphon House. Plus, God allowed me to write for some Korean publishers, too! A friend at church told me she was an editor/writer at an English publisher in Seoul, and when she found out I was a writer, she asked if I could help edit some English books for them. Via email, she sent me work — editing English books for middle school students in Korea. This was a whole new experience, and I really enjoyed it, learning how Koreans studied English.

Also, advertized in my freelance job board was another publisher in Seoul with an office in California, who was looking for educational writers for guided reading books. My previous work for Lakeshore Learning helped me in this endeavor. I ended up writing ten guided reading books for them. And one of the books with my name on it was sent to the Bologna Children's Book Fair, as a sample for the publisher. Wow! Little by little, God added to my repertoire and supplied an extra income.

Sharing My Testimony

Living in a foreign country and writing hasn't all been glorious.

Loneliness or homesickness would set in and still does. But God spoke to my heart to "bloom where I'm planted." And He used the example of Moses in the Bible. Moses was a Hebrew, raised as an Egyptian. In Exodus 9:16 God told Moses, "I have raised you up for this very purpose, that I might show you my power and that my name might be proclaimed in all the earth." I didn't know how long we'd be in Korea. I kept asking God, "Why am I here? What am I supposed to do?" I know God has a plan and a purpose, and He continues to reveal that to me. So I decided to share my testimony. Every day, I receive emailed devotions from The Upper Room. So, I decided to send them three devotions that I'd written. They chose the one with my testimony of living in another country, and it was published in August 2013. It encouraged many, and I was so thankful. My prayer now is that people would be blessed through my writing and testimony.

A Dilemma

During my second year in Korea, an American friend who taught at an international school in another city in Korea asked if I wanted to teach at their school. This would've been an awesome opportunity for my children to attend there free, but I knew I wouldn't be able to both write and teach. Plus, we'd have to move away from my father-in-law. So my husband and I prayed about it, and I asked God to clearly show us His will. That week I received three work-for-hire book contracts. I guess God wanted me to continue writing. And I was very glad.

God's Provision

God provided for some of my loneliness problems through my joining other children's writers in a Facebook group called 12x12. This was a challenge and idea of Julie Hedlund, a Colorado writer, that we write one picture book draft every month. In our Facebook group we became a family and shared our writing journeys and tips. I've grown in my craft just by being with them. And the group continues to grow each year. From this 12x12 group, I joined another online picture book critique group with writers in the U.S.,

New Zealand, and France. They have been such an encouragement to me and have really boosted my writing. I've also taken some online picture book writing classes and had professional critiques via Skype and the Internet phone. Being on the other side of the world didn't seem to matter so much anymore as long as I had the Internet. And where did God place me? In the world's second fastest Internet country. Thank you, God!

I also started writing for an educational content provider called QBS. They needed freelance educational writers for various projects. They didn't care where in the world I lived, as long as I had the Internet! I've learned so much from writing for various clients in all sorts of grade levels through them. They hosted live online meetings that I was able to attend via my computer. They were impressed that I woke up at ungodly hours in the morning or the middle of the night to be in the meetings.

Writing about Culture

Living in Korea has given me a plethora of ideas for children's books. I have a few manuscripts waiting to find a home with a publisher. One is dear to my heart as it has to do with North Korean refugee children. When I first heard about their plight at church, it tugged on my heart. I researched online and read about these refugees living in Korea and abroad. I found the name of one of the masterminds behind the Asian Underground Railroad and, through a translator (my husband), interviewed him and two North Korean refugee children. I hope this book finds a home soon and can help open the eyes of the world to these children so they can receive all the help they need.

Every month it seems like Korea has a holiday, and my children and I can't keep them straight, especially because Korea uses the lunar calendar. I discovered Tuttle Publishing in Vermont (U.S.) and saw they published books about Asia. In their children's section they had a small series about holidays in Japan and the Philippines. So I emailed them my idea to do a book on Korean holidays and celebrations. Six months later, I was asked to send them a book proposal. The editor told me she liked the proposal. But publishing is slow, and it was only two years later that she emailed saying she was ready to pursue this book idea. Hooray! This will be my first royalty-paying picture book, not work-for-hire. This would never have happened if God hadn't moved us to Korea. Furthermore, she gave my name to an editor in Singapore, where Tuttle Publishing also has an office. I'll be revising a work-for-hire project for them — writing activities for Korean language flashcards. Once again, my teaching background has come in handy.

Bloom Where I'm Planted

I continue to write, learn, and connect with others through social media. And through my blog, Korean writers have contacted me! I met one of them, a lady who is also a member of the SCBWI. She told me of an upcoming event hosted at a library in Seoul. The American author Rosemary Wells was presenting about children's writing! For the first time, I took the subway by myself into Seoul and met this Korean writer. She was a gracious host and, through her limited English and Google translator, we were able to communicate. Since I haven't been able to attend SCBWI meetings and there isn't a Korea SCBWI, I had a wonderful time listening to what Rosemary had to say.

> Little eyes are always watching me as I compose stories, sitting at my computer day in and day out. What do my children think of me?

Just a couple of weeks ago, a Korean American contacted me to say that she was moving back to Korea and wanted to join a writing group. Will there be a Korean SCBWI again? Perhaps.

A Legacy

Little eyes are always watching me as I compose stories, sitting at my computer day in and day out. What do my children think of me? They've told me I work hard and they like my stories. Often they are my first editors. And I've seen their own writing blossom as I homeschool them while in Korea. I pray my writing touches their hearts and that they would walk with God all their lives.

As I've given my writing for God's glory, He has helped and led me every step of the way. I pray for ideas and for strength and creativity when I'm on assignments. And God never fails. I love the story of Ezra in the Bible; how God's hand was on him because he "devoted himself to the study and observance of the Law of the Lord..." (Ezra 7:10). I know God's hand is on everything I do, even the little things.

As a writer in Asia, God has lifted me up and allowed me to influence others in writing. People email and tell me how I've helped them. Being one of the only few writers from South Korea in my Facebook groups makes me stick out like a sore thumb. Maybe that's a good thing. I'm excited for future projects God has planned for me. To God be the glory.

THE GLORIOUS JOURNEY THAT I ENJOY MUCH

ABU TAHER CHOWDHURY of Nepal has been blessed with opportunities to try his hand at many different areas of ministry. From being a missionary, he went on to be a writer of stories and articles, an editor, a composer of devotional songs and also a publisher. He now serves as the Chairman of the Enlightened Society of Bangladesh and is the Principal of Creative Jewels School & College.

How To Be Saved was printed on the cover of a booklet. There was a picture of a young boy holding on to window bars and weeping. In 1973, when I was studying in a *madrasah* (religious school), I saw some people gathered around a white man and his two young Bengali friends at a nearby road. I walked towards them and saw the booklet in their hands. I was told that it was part of a gospel packet which also included some tracts. I paid 10 paisa to buy it. The boy on the cover seemed to me to be imprisoned in the house. There didn't seem to be anyone to set him free. I thought he had been kidnapped. Once, in my boyhood, I was almost kidnapped by some thugs but, fortunately, I was saved by my neighbors. I was so frightened by the experience that I didn't go out of my home for a month.

I was born into a conservative family who were followers of one of the major world religions. I had to live under so many rules and regulations that I thought I was in prison. So I could identify with the boy on the cover and wondered if there might be a message for me inside the booklet. I was curious about the booklet and tracts in the package because I knew they had been written by Christians. I did not like any other religion apart from my own. In fact, I used to hate Christians as I had heard that their teachings were false and went against Allah. But the booklet broke the unbreakable boundary of my heart and opened a new door to me.

First Bitter Experience Reading Books

I bought the packet, brought it into the *madrasah* and skimmed through the booklet and tracts. I couldn't read all of them because the other curious students were excited to see the Christian material and took them all away from me, except for the first booklet. They wanted to take that away from me too, but I wouldn't let them. The tracts were like fast food for the hungry children. They didn't seem to care about religious boundaries. They read and made various comments. Most of them were saying good things about the tracts. Unfortunately, word got round to the head teacher and I was called to the office. I had to submit the booklet to the principal and so did the other students. The principal asked a lot of questions: How dare I bring these prohibited books into the *madrasah*? What made me do that? Did I buy them or were they given to me at no cost? Did they give me money to use the material to destroy our religion? After a long monologue, I was severely beaten by two of my teachers as I couldn't answer the questions to their satisfaction. Then the principal called my home tutor who was also one of the teachers in the same *madrasah* and instructed him to pass a message, along with the booklets, to my parents. So he did, and I was beaten again at home.

Negative Attitude Created Curiosity

I was personally not very fond of books. Reading anything was boring for me. Whenever I opened a book my eyelids would become tired and I would fall asleep. Books could never draw my attention. I was not even interested in the books I had to study in class. But I had to read them, otherwise I would be punished, both at home and at school. But now, the reverse was happening. I was puzzled... *What is in the booklet that they don't want me to read? There must be something important.*

> I was puzzled...
> What is in the
> booklet that they
> don't want me to
> read? There must
> be something
> important.

I kept watch in case those people came again to sell their books by the roadside, but they never appeared. Once I was at a nearby market to buy vegetables and saw the same young people with a white missionary and they were selling gospel packets again. I grabbed the chance to buy another packet. I was happy I could make the purchase but soon became upset when I recalled what had recently happened. I thought of ways to avoid another beating. I carefully hid the books inside my shirt, took them home and kept them under a wooden box. After a month, I had a chance to look through the booklet. I discovered that Christian books were not that harmful. They actually spoke of hope and freedom. Unfortunately,

I didn't have a chance to read the booklet fully. During the time they were kept under the box, rats and cockroaches had feasted on them. I was very upset by that. Fortunately, there was an address and I became hopeful of buying the books again. However, the fear of being caught and beaten again was always there.

A Safe Place to Read

How could I get those books again? I didn't know what to do because although there was an address still visible on the torn booklet, I didn't know the place and the city was not familiar to me. One day, I gathered up enough courage to go to Chittagong City where there was a Christian library. I found two young men who welcomed me with smiling faces. They were very friendly and helped me to find the books. I read the first booklet again at that secure place. I read books for the whole day. I neither felt bored nor drowsy. I was so happy to read more and more. The books really opened my eyes. I felt that someone was knocking at the door of my heart and was personally talking to me. I discovered that I was the person who was really in bondage. I clearly understood that in my current situation I had no hope of going to heaven. Was hell my future destination? I was overwhelmed by thoughts of what my future would have been like if I hadn't read the booklet. For the first time I realized how powerful a book can be!

Books Can Change Lives

I fell in love with books. By returning again and again to that library, I read many of the books and tracts for six whole months. I went to the library twice or thrice a week. One of the books I read was titled *Asha-Alo-Jibon* (Hope-Light-Life) and discussed many issues like the Son of God, Jesus' death and resurrection, and His second coming. After a year, my friends gave me a Bible. The language was very hard to understand. I thought it was written for Hindus and tribal people. But after three weeks of reading, I discovered an awesomely rich new world. My friends subsequently invited me to attend a church where I could sing songs and listen to various people speaking. It was so good. Here was a place where

I could get answers for many of the questions that had been raised in my mind during the times I spent reading at the library. I began to join weekly prayer meetings and attended church on a regular basis. On one occasion, my parents and relatives found out about my weekly adventures and I was again beaten severely.

My Christian friends became anxious for me and for the security of the library. Finally, they sent me to Chandpur Baptist Church on July 2, 1976. This was about 200 kilometers away from my home. I was introduced to a pastor named Ashish Adhikery who helped me to study the books of Luke and John so that I could understand more about salvation and new birth. On August 2, I finally confessed my sins to God and invited Jesus into my life. Oh, what joy and peace filled my mind and heart! I was taught from the book of Romans for the next week. Following that, I was baptized on August 10.

> I fell in love with books. By returning again and again to that library, I read many of the books and tracts for six whole months.

I immediately became concerned for my loved ones. I felt that my parents and other family members were similarly in bondage and hopeless like I had been. I closed my eyes and the faces of all of my dear ones flashed through my mind. What would happen to them? I realized only an appropriate book and its life-giving message could open their hearts. I vowed there and then to be a writer of books which would lead people to the source of life. Only problem was, I didn't know the ABCs of writing. Basically, I was not a bright student, and it was difficult for me to even spell more difficult words. I could not speak well as I had problems with proper pronunciation. But that booklet gave me new courage through its simple unspoken message — "Books can change lives."

I Became a Book Hawker

I spent time praying and asking to learn to write books. After some time, God brought me an opportunity to join the Operation Mobilization (OM) team. I was so excited to see the young people who were selling books in the marketplace with great enthusiasm and power. They would go out in four teams: foot team, boat team, vehicle team, and bicycle team. I heard many stories about their courage in going to the district office, court building, secretariats and other large offices. I realized that God was guiding and leading me to be an author for His Kingdom. With great excitement, I joined the team in a local seminar.

The normal practice would be for us to study at the station. We studied the Bible individually and in groups, memorized verses, shared ideas, and discussed questions with the Bible as our source of answers. Out in the public square, however, we would often be questioned by the people who bought our books. Most of the time, I struggled to answer the questions and, on one occasion, I thought that I would have to leave the team, but the Holy Spirit impressed upon me not to. Actually, this was our practical field study where we saw firsthand people's emotions and stresses, affection and anger, love and hatred. We also collected new ideas and songs from different places and shared them with one another.

One day in 1980, a voice inside my heart said, "Why don't you write down what you have learnt?" With that prompting, I started writing a course called *Tarika Hok* (The True Way). It was the fruit of my practical field training. Whenever we walked in the villages, people would ask us questions. Sometimes there would be agreement with our answers and the people would be happy. Other times, there would be disagreements and some even quarreled with us. One thing came through very clearly — they wanted to know the real truth. I could see the great thirst in their eyes. When I was writing the course I kept photos of those people I had talked to close by. When it was completed, I asked some friends to vet it. By making the necessary corrections according to their comments and suggestions, I became more confident. It was appreciated by the Bible school who took copies for their use. At this point, I decided that I would write more books for the sake of my people.

A Milestone

I once spent days and nights writing a poem and a feature article. When I finally thought that they were good enough, I sent them to *Nobojug* magazine. This is a well-known Christian magazine published by the New Zealand Baptist Mission. I thought that my poem and article would be published in time and I would have my copy. I waited for months but I didn't get any response. I wrote letters to them, but no answer. I became upset and finally wrote another letter requesting that they let me know what was wrong with my writings. When I still received no answer for months, I decided to write another poem and sent it again to *Nobojug*. Just after I had sent it, I received a letter of apology from the editor of *Nobojug*. He also included a corrected copy of my first poem. "You have good writing skills," he said, "but you need to be careful about your spelling and choice of words, illustrations and title." He also suggested that I consider reading some modern poetry.

One day in 1980, a voice inside my heart said, "Why don't you write down what you have learnt?"

Though I did not agree with all his points, I learnt a lot from his comments, corrections and suggestions. I learnt how to improve myself. I was so excited that I didn't care about food, and didn't hesitate to spend the whole day and night improving my poem. The following morning, I sent it off again to the editor. This time, he wrote back to say, "Bravo, Taher! I am very happy that you are on the right track. Now go ahead and send your poems and rhymes each month. I'll see what I can do, but don't forget to read others' poetry." He also invited me to participate in a writer seminar the following month. I was so thrilled and that was one of the milestones in my journey.

New Fields of Writing

In 1982, I was invited to work with the Bangladesh Bible Correspondence School under the Association of Baptists for World Evangelism (ABWE) in Chittagong. After spending a couple of months in thought and prayer, I left the OM team to join the School. I am delighted to say that God led me to fulfill His purposes. It was another training field for me. I had to check the correspondence courses and answer many questions sent in by inquirers. Though I later became the principal of the Bible School, I never forgot my gift of writing; I took it as an opportunity to do more. I realized that I was yet a baby in the field of writing and I needed to learn a lot more to establish myself. I was glad to be introduced to Mr. George Weber and Mr. Larry Allen, missionaries with ABWE. They were gracious in their fellowship and thoughtful in their teaching of the Word of God. They showed me how to discover and mine the resources from the Bible. I was encouraged by them to study the Bible personally and also in the Baptist Bible Institute in Bangladesh (BBIB). By learning more from the Word of God I would have a foundation as an author in the Kingdom of God.

Soon, I came to know that the ABWE had a Literature Division. When I visited I was excited to see all the different books that I had been looking for. Later I met a lady named Jeannie Lockerbie; a skilled trainer, a perfect organizer, and a successful author. As she was the director of the Literature Division, she became a mentor in my writing journey for some years when I worked as a magazine editor at the Division. She encouraged me to translate daily devotionals. That was another opportunity to learn how to write and set new and appropriate illustrations. Through the devotionals that I translated for six years, called *Amader Dainik Ahar* (Our Daily Bread), I realized that I was on the road to learning what it means to be an author. Miss Jeannie was a living blessing in my journey. It was she who encouraged me to participate in various workshops and seminars in Bangladesh, India and England to develop my skill. She also inspired me to attend an MAI conference in Hertfordshire, near London, in 1993. I cannot begin to describe how encouraged and blessed I was by the various participants in that workshop! I believe that God added that opportunity to gear me up in my journey.

New Needs in Churches

In those days, I was also involved in Church ministry as an elected deacon. I noticed that the church was gradually dwindling. People were becoming less interested in participating in worship. Young people didn't have anything to do. The same sermons were being repeated and people often napped. Old songs didn't mean anything to the worshipers and the young people were feeling discouraged. I told the deacons' committee that I would like to help the young people. That was how I was selected to be the leader of the youth group.

> Dr. Olsen made us realize that high-quality literature can be useful for the elites both inside and outside the church, but useless for the vast majority of the target audience. I learnt a great lesson: *I have to use language carefully in any kind of writing.*

I started to use *Our Daily Bread* twice a week. God then led me to write dramas for different seasons. I composed new songs when there was a need and I practiced them with the youth. I encouraged them to write something for posting on the church notice board. They were impressed and happy. I saw how things changed within a year. Later, I composed songs for devotions on personal faith, Christmas, Easter, the Resurrection, marriage ceremonies, etc., and most of them were much appreciated by the youth group as well as other members of the church. I was so happy and grateful to God that some of the songs found their way into the church's worship songbook.

Appropriate Language

Sometime later, I met a man of God called Dr. Viggo B. Olsen. He had gracious-looking eyes, and a kind voice. It was his enduring love and keen observations which helped me much as an author and translator. He was the author of the bestseller *Daktar: Diplomat in Bangladesh* and had also published a common-language Bengali version of the Bible for the majority community in Bangladesh. This translation changed the history of 200 years. We had an older version of the Bible which had been translated by William Yates and William Carey. It was a good translation for Indians as well as for the minority community (idol worshippers) in Bangladesh. But for the Muslims who made up 85 percent of Bangladesh's population, it was inappropriate. We had no other choice but to use that translation even though a lot of questions arose in people's minds when using it in church or personally. That is why the Muslims rejected it for 200 years. When I was doing fieldwork in the OM team, I experienced firsthand how people reacted. Most of them would receive the Bible in their hands with a big smile. However, when they opened it and saw that the very first word was *Ishawr* (God) rather than *Allah*, their faces would darken. They would close the book, return it to us, and then quickly run away. Not only that, the language level of the Carey Bible (like the King James Version) was pitched at more highly educated people, whereas the average language level of the people is 5th to 8th grade. In the church the situation was similar to that in the Muslim community, where the Quran was only for *mawlawis* (teachers) to understand and not for the general populace. Dr. Olsen made us realize that high-quality literature can be useful for the elites both inside and outside the church, but useless for the vast majority of the target audience. I learnt a great lesson: *I have to use language carefully in any kind of writing*. After this translation, thousands of copies were sold and still continue to be sold. I clearly remember, when I was in the OM team in 1982, our whole team of 30 people used to sell 50-100 copies of the Carey Bible per month. After the new translation was published, however, we sold thousands of copies per day. What a change! Just unbelievable! Praise God.

My Calling as an Editor

In 1987 I was called to be an editor of a magazine called *Ittyadi*. It was Miss Jeannie Lockerbie (now Mrs. Stephenson) who encouraged me to take up that position. She somehow discovered that I would be suitable for the role. This was my golden time of learning again how to write stories, novels, dramas and poems. Every day, I had to read various kinds of writing and needed to edit them. At the same time, I also had to write something for each issue of the magazine. I was badly criticized for my writing, yet received many encouraging letters too. I learnt to receive criticism and it became a part of my learning process. My world of writing expanded.

> I disliked the title and avoided reading it as I thought that it was not a smart title at all. How could it be the title of a book? Who would read it?

Every day, apart from my editing work, I had to face people too. I knew that many of them had been exposed to half-truths about Christianity. Well, a half-truth is not a truth at all, but they would still come to us and try to debate. We would spend hours debating. It came to the point where I felt that I had to collect all the topics of our debates and answer them with the real truth from the Word of God. That was how I ended up writing *Unknown Truth*. It became quite popular with those who were actively seeking the Truth.

Opportunity to Study in a Seminary

I graduated with a degree in the Arts in 1987. According to our educational system, for an Arts degree I had to study various subjects, e.g., history, economics, political science, Bangla literature, etc. Bangla literature was my favorite subject. By studying the Holy Bible, I learnt that it has many elements of literature. I was thrilled by how the authors of the different Bible books wrote such attractive narratives with their God-given skill. I fell in love with the Bible and was hungry to study the Word of

God properly. I prayed, and also requested others to pray for me.

In 1990, God answered my prayers and I had a chance to study in Bangladesh Theological Seminary which is affiliated with Northwest Baptist Seminary in the USA. That was a golden time of my life. God brought me a dozen godly people during my period of study who were highly educated and skilled. I met some very devoted pastors too who taught me in the seminary. They became my role models and impacted me greatly. I learnt how the godly authors of the Holy Bible wrote stories, histories, poems, lectures, dialogues, songs, proverbs, and letters.

The Importance of a Title

In 1998 I left my position as an editor and started to give more time to familiarizing myself with the book business in terms of the various kinds of books and readers. I had the opportunity to meet many readers. They used to share their feelings with me, and would ask if I knew which books would be good for them and which not. Being a bookseller, I reviewed thousands of titles. Though I didn't have enough time and patience to read them all, I had some idea of what was in the books and could easily make general suggestions.

There was a time when I decided to study the titles of books. I was surprised by the smart titles that some authors came up with and how people were attracted to them. I once bought a book titled *Mouchake Dhil* (Throwing Stones at a Hive). I disliked the title and avoided reading it as I thought that it was not a smart title at all. How could it be the title of a book? Who would read it? But the distributor insisted that I should take three copies. I thought that it would be useless and left idle on the shelf. One day, however, I noticed five customers looking for that book. My curiosity grew and made me want to read it. After reading the first couple of lines, I continued to read every single word of the book in one sitting. After that, I came to the conclusion that the title was indeed appropriate and splendid! That day, I learned the importance of a good title.

Relevance for Secular Study

The training and guidance that I received from the people of God was not only helpful for my spiritual life but for all of life. In 1999, I established a school called Creative Jewels. I composed a theme song for Creative Jewels and it became very popular. I also composed parade songs and some other seasonal songs, as well as rhymes for elementary, primary, middle and high school students. Watching their enjoyment makes me happy. I also wrote a phonics book and two grammar books for elementary students.

My Call to Publishing

In 1994 a friend of mine by the name of Dr. Paul Thomas invited me to assist him in starting a publishing ministry. He was a missionary from the USA. He was devoted to reaching the majority community of Bangladesh. Since I had also come to Christ from that community, his ministry drew my attention. Through my work with him, I found out that even though he was a Science graduate and highly educated, yet he lived a very simple life, and ate very simple food like the village people in Bangladesh. He was always keen to learn things from others, walking in the villages, asking questions, and spending time with the villagers. He learnt how to walk, talk, dress, and entertain others in the Bengali way. I saw how everybody loved and honored him. He was and is a living book for me. I saw him writing and editing courses. They were so good and attractive. Although I was familiar with the traditional religious and social customs, I still needed to know how to present the message of God to the unsaved people in a simple and effective way.

> I saw that God wants us to present His Words in our own language, culture and context by using our skills.

We finally formed an organization called "*Shikka Kolyan* Trust" (Learning for Living Educational Welfare Trust) and I became the chairman of the organization. The aim of the organization was to publish books and courses for the majority community of Bangladeshi people. I realized that God had been working in my life to use the writing skills He had provided me. I saw, in my journey through the Word of God, how He used different kinds of people with different skills to write His Words in the Bible. I was so happy to serve in the organization. We had monthly meetings to review major issues and decisions. I had a limited opportunity to take care of the practical side of things. In 2004, God called me to be the director of SKT as well as the principal of Agape Theological College in the same organization. During my service I took care of the editing of all kinds of literature. I translated books and courses, and I edited tracts, booklets and books. I saw that God wants us to present His Words in our own language, culture and context by using our skills.

Persecution

In the OM team I had learnt how to distribute and sell books. In SKT we published books but didn't have time to distribute them. I therefore encouraged the staff and Agape College students to distribute books to the garment factory workers and at the market places. This way, we were able to sell hundreds of books and distribute thousands of tracts and booklets every month.

Many times, however, we were persecuted for distributing books. Sometimes people would beat us, sometimes they would burn our books and drive us away. It wasn't all bad, though; we had good experiences too. We would sometimes meet people who liked us. They not only bought books, but encouraged others to buy, and would serve us tea, coffee, and food. Some others even rescued us from nasty people. They appeared to us like angels. I thank God for using our books for His glory.

During the process of distribution, I discovered some errors: pictures of Jesus and the prophets, and some statements which we could avoid to reduce unnecessary confusion among the readers. I learnt how necessary it is to deliver timely messages and the priority we should give it. I learnt why it is necessary to write things in an orderly and careful way in books. I came to understand that God trains his people in practical ways, like He did with Moses and David.

My Present Ministry

In 2006, I was invited to interpret for a foreigner called Mr. Dan Scheel from the US. I was thrilled to listen to his marvelous testimony and teaching. Although he was a well-established businessman, he sold everything and left all for the sake of the Kingdom of God. He became a student of the Bible and, even though he never went to a Bible College nor any seminary, he had a tremendous teaching ministry. I saw him teaching from a series called *Firm Foundations* for hours at a time. He was about 70 but I never saw him tired. He honored the Word of God. He never forgot to mention the right verse in the right place. He emphasized the importance of the Bible and insisted on the congregation using their own Bibles. I liked that.

Though I was more accustomed to topical teaching, I liked his teaching from *Firm Foundations* which was written to teach the Bible in chronological order. I didn't know about Chronological Bible Teaching Ministry International (CBTMI) prior to this. But I thanked God for the organization, because I felt that they provided a proper understanding of God's message. However, as I was involved in a different method of teaching, I didn't say anything. Instead, God opened my eyes to other opportunities. I saw the children's edition of *Firm Foundations* and that gave me the idea to adapt this for our ministry as we didn't have good enough materials for children in SKT.

Recent Inspiration

I realize that we serve a God who has blessed us with much creativity. Our call is to make ourselves available. Recently I was inspired to write and compose new songs for the glory of the Lord. King David was a well-known author and composer of songs in the

Bible. He composed, collected, edited, and sang hundreds of songs. He collected songs from very ancient times as well as modern. He collected various solo, duet and group songs. But he was not satisfied with all he had done. He suggested that his listeners compose new songs (Psalm 33:3; 47:7). His endless hunger and thirst (Psalm 42:1,2; 143:6) for God led him to write and collect more and more songs till the end of his life. At the end of the book of Psalms (149:1), he again encouraged others to write new songs so the ongoing process of writing songs for the Lord might continue forever and ever. Isaiah also told us to write new songs (Isaiah 42:10). What it taught me is that God continues to inspire creative musicians to compose new songs for His glory. All this encouraged me to try setting the songs of Psalms to new music. God willing, I hope to publish a songbook for His glory.

IN HIS HANDS

TIN DINH of Vietnam has been writing
creatively since she was a young girl.
Through the transitions of her life, writing
continued to provide her with a source of
solace, a means of reflection and a channel
of obedience to the Father who never
left her comfortless. Her strong sense of
perfectionism has seen her successfully
heading up the editorial/writing team
of a women's magazine, and editing a
compilation of heartwarming testimonies to
God's great love and mercy.

Growing Up

I'm the youngest daughter in a family of four siblings. My mother gave birth to me when everyone thought she was already past childbearing age. I often wondered if that was the reason I received the nickname "scrawny"? I used to really hate that name. But mom never seemed to be bothered at all. What was worse was having to listen to the oft-repeated "Back then I was afraid I wouldn't be able to give birth to her at such an age, so I took Chinese medicine. That's why she came out tiny but tough like a stick." Already being very self-conscious about my "withered" look, I felt even more ashamed every time people laughed upon hearing my mom's story.

In those days, I used to hate looking in the mirror or having photographs taken, and I would be embarrassed each time someone looked at me. In contrast, I loved so dearly the scenery around me. We had a wooden home on a hill in DaLat; a place where we didn't even need to lock the door when we went out. The howling sound of the wind through the pines is deeply imprinted in my memory. Every morning, looking out from the window I could see the fresh green of leaves upon rolling mountains. The environment was so peaceful and quiet that you could hear even the sound of the chicken and the bird flapping their wings.

My childhood was filled with trees, plants, and the scent of leaves. And the friends I used to hang out with back in those days were a group of minority kids whose veins were pumping with the vigor of the wild. We used to climb hills to pick mushrooms, or go sledding on dry pine leaves down the steep slopes. Other times we would be wading (sometimes stumbling) our way through small rocky streams. Those kids always went barefoot while I would try to drag along my oversized sandals, which kept slipping off my tiny feet. (In order to save money, my mom usually bought me clothes that were larger than my actual size so they would last me longer as I grew into them.) Even though those kids cracked up every time I tripped and fell, I still loved being in their company.

Come Sunday, though, it was a totally different situation. I could no longer be me while standing among my church friends who were dressed up nicely. Looking at their neatly combed hair with colorful bows and hair-bands, I felt ashamed because of my short, sunbleached and unevenly trimmed hair. I felt even more out of place wearing the loose hand-me-down pants from my sister among all the pretty dresses that the other girls were wearing. And I still remember how much it hurt my heel each time I took a step in those hard tennis shoes. Therefore each Sunday, when I left my own little haven, I would feel like a small turtle that only wants to hide away in its rough and rugged shell.

Ironically, Sunday, my favorite day of the week, was also the day that I hated. I liked it because I could go to town and to church, playing, singing, and listening to stories. But I hated it because I had to face the thing that made my childhood heavy — a sense of inferiority on account of my poor and ugly state.

All I needed during those times was a piece of paper to write down my feelings when I couldn't tell anybody.

What I'm telling you might seem long-winded, but that was how I grew up. The sadness and the happiness were all mixed up together. But the happiness was far greater and I'm still able to feel it. The sadness was not worth holding on to. All I needed during those times was a piece of paper to write down my feelings when I couldn't tell anybody. After I was done writing, if it was a nice and square piece of paper, I would fold it into a little boat. But if it was an ugly piece taken from the calendar or scrap paper, I would crumple it and throw it away.

And so I continued to grow up. My teen years were unforgettable. I often wondered why the mischievousness in me grew faster than my body. Although I was the smallest among my peers, I was often the naughtiest. I learned to combine my playfulness with my hobby of writing to "pass on the inspiration" to my close friends. So, whenever we had a joint Sunday morning service, I would pass round a small piece of paper to my friends. On it, each of us would write a line and, together, we came up with many horrific *haikus*. They were in a five-word format with proper rhymes. But the main subjects of our collaboration ranged from a kid with missing teeth, a guy with poorly combed hair, to even highly respected figures such as our pastor. The deacon of the church also became our favorite subject for our compilation, and we were all hugging each other and laughing to ourselves. I am sure none of our parents knew about this.

Winds of Change

The year 1975 saw many political changes in our country. And, more or less, the changes also impacted me. My two brothers and my brother-in-law, due to their association with the old government, were pushed to a penitentiary. My neighborhood became even quieter because the minority population in our area was also relocated to a new economic region.

As for me, I had to leave my favorite school, which was nestled on a beautiful hillside, and move to another nearby school that looked like a poor, dirty apartment. Each day I had to drag with me to school a hoe and a broom. And so each day went by... I sadly witnessed the dreamlike beauty of DaLat fading away. Our pretty flower bushes now had to give way to potato beds; and the soothing silence was broken by the Red music obnoxiously ringing from speakers hung along the streets, "...headed to Saigon, we'll wipe out the enemies...."

It seemed to me that even the pines had stopped singing during those days, and the flowers of the seasons also seemed dead. My innocence had also left without me noticing. I felt bitter when the church turned into a place where believers could no longer gather freely. And I was really scared when I heard the news that our pastor had been arrested. The threat of the church being shut down was a constant fear hanging over my head.

During that time, there were so many reasons for me to ask God why he allowed these things to happen. I had to live with an anger that could not be appeased. But I was no longer a child who could just write down my feelings on little pieces of paper, crumple them, and toss away as I used to. Now, however, I had my own diary. It's a great comfort to have a spotless little friend always ready for me to pour out my all secrets — the interesting, sad, and even boring moments in my life.

I wrote my diary every day but never thought about what I would do with it. Seasons went by year after year, but all my stories remained on the pages. I kept on writing, sometimes just a few words or a few sentences, but some other times a few pages. Oddly enough, I never bothered to read what I had written.

The day came when a new season dawned in my life. I had to gather all my personal belongings in preparation for a move... I was going to get married. It was a rainy day, so I had the whole day just to read through all my diaries of various sizes, from thick to thin — the ones that had been with me at every turn along my journey. It was mind-boggling! It was as if I were watching a very emotional movie. As I turned the pages, I sometimes had to stop to cry, to laugh, and to thank God for seeing me through the past 18 years in the mists of the foggy mountains. Only when I was mature enough did He bring me to the biggest city in the country, where he kept me safe in the midst of all kinds of temptations. He eventually placed my hand in the hand of the one in whom, He knew, I would find love, care, and comfort for the rest of my life.

My husband is the only person who has had a chance to read what I had written. He carefully gathered my diaries and kept them in a safe place. He said, "Years from now when we're old, you'll have a lot of fun reading them again." I have never written in another diary since.

Life of various colors — bright and dark — continues to go by. God blessed us with many opportunities and advantages as we journeyed through this new season of life together. I had a warm home, loving husband, cute son, good-paying job, in addition to many other blessings. I felt like I was at the peak of joy and peace. But the foolishness of every human is acting as if they no longer need God when life becomes easy. It's sad that I was one of them. The more I built my life, the further I drifted away from God. The cycle of life kept sucking me in so relentlessly that the image of God began to fade away. Going to church every Sunday became a routine.

However, God's love continued to pursue me! He had wonderful ways of not letting me slip away.

I remember back in my childhood, God had taught me through the fascinating flora and fauna around me: from the thin wings of the butterflies to the closing petals of the *Mimosa Pudica* each time I touched it. How can I tell enough of God's presence with me in those days? Then, with wonder, He showed me His loving protection though my difficult years. But now...now, I had to learn about God in a most unexpected way. I went from the peak into the valley.

Those were extremely stressful times. My husband and I had to face many unexpected difficulties in our business; loss and trickery assaulted us from many directions. We were surrounded by so much trouble that I used to wake up with feelings of anxiety and distress. I wondered what might come next? However, I counted them as unavoidable misfortunes in life.

Pressures continued to prolong and drain me. One day, I found that I could not get up — tuberculosis had made its home into my lungs. On my sick bed, I remember thinking to myself, *Could it be that all these troubles, hardship and sickness didn't just occur by chance? What if they are messages from God? What if He earnestly wants to tell me something?* But yet we still tried our best to organize the chaos surrounding us. My husband sought out connections to help resolve our business problems. We also learned to avoid further losses by becoming more careful in dealing with people. And I received medical care from one of the top doctors in the field. Time went by, and the storm was calmed. I had thought that with my own strength I would be able to manage everything! But I was dead wrong.

The day I realized that I did not have control over my life the way I wanted to, was also the day I came face to face with another tragic truth — I could not save my newborn twin daughters whom I had carried for nearly eight months. For the first time in my life, I truly understood pain. I felt so small, weak, and helpless!

After days lying face down on my tear-soaked pillow, I began to understand. God is loving and He is also just. He does not give me all that I want, but all that I need. Therefore, He walked with me through the deep valleys so I can grow up and understand *the* important thing: God can give me everything, but He can also take them all away if He wants to. I really possess nothing in this world! This was a valuable lesson that I will remember as long as I live.

> The trainer's words kept ringing in my head, "A message on the page can spread and bring change to many lives."

It's a shame that I used to blame God. But there's none who is as patient with me as He is. Just like a great sculptor, He has been shaping me through each trial. This has happened so many times that my point of view has changed. I no longer deal with life's troubles in the same way. I know that He has waited long, very long indeed, to hear the change in my prayer, from "God, I want you to do this and that for me," to "Lord, I want to do something for you." How can I be indifferent knowing that the One who created billions of universes would care for the troubles in my life, big or small? God works quietly but powerfully; He is far yet so near. Many times, I've been overwhelmed by joy and tears as I experienced His wonderful hand upon my small family. With each new day, His love continued to melt away the ice in me, and the prayer "I want to do something for you" continued to ring out every time I knelt to pray.

I truly wanted to do something more. But I did not know what it should be.

In 2008, in God's divine provision, I received a phone call from a very close friend (she was also one of those who collaborated with me on my horrifying *haikus* when we were young). That was how I was connected to a writing workshop conducted by Media Associates International (MAI).

I enjoyed coming to this class because I had a chance to meet with many other sisters who had a lot in common with me. We talked and laughed, but I never thought it would be the starting point of an opportunity to do something for God.

The term "writing" is not something new to me, but I never seriously considered it as a vocation. And that brief training workshop could never be sufficient to equip someone to become a writer. However, God's ways are always unique. He used simple tips to stir up in me something powerful. The trainer's words kept ringing in my head, "A message on the page can spread and bring change to many lives." *Wow, what can be more amazing than that!* I was very encouraged. Although I'd been a believer all my life, the number of those "lucky" people who heard about God through me was very small. I have always been ashamed of this. But what a great idea to lead people to God through the tip of your pen. I was so excited, I shouted in my head, *Yes! I'll write! I will write.*

In my mind, I had planned to write about the lives that had been touched and transformed by God. Personally speaking, I had learned about God in the church pew, but really grew and was transformed by the evidence of His work. He is present here and now, walking along the bumpy road of life and listening to the prayers of those in despair. His hand is ready to uplift the weak and heal the sick (including me). I had such amazing things to write about.

It was interesting that after only a few days of training, we sisters, who only knew how to use chopsticks, could now express our ideas with pens. The very first issue of our magazine came out during Christmas of 2008. Praise be to God!

I would like to say to the members of MAI (including those far away that we did not have the honor to meet) that their effort has borne fruit.

As for me, it was just the beginning.

I had never ever thought that I would write something for many to read. That would not have been me — a person who grew up with a sense of inferiority and who used to clam up around people. But, after all that had happened, God had awoken something buried deep within. He has motivated me to go to faraway places and meet with people that I've never known before. I have listened to them, prayed with them, and gone over their lives with pen and paper through both their joys and tears. And the amazing thing I have gained after each meeting with these simple-but-special individuals is that I get to learn more about God. And my love for Him grows deeper.

> I no longer write alone like before, but now I'm blessed to write with the One who chose and called me to this task.

God is amazing. He gradually grew my confidence with each passing day of writing. He helped me to love and feel the joy or pain of others as if they were my own. I could enter into the feelings of cold and loneliness of a person who had recently lost a family member, or jump for joy because somebody was saved. That sense of empathy helps me to write about other people in such way that even they sob while reading it.

I thank God that He made possible the impossible. I'm now writing quietly and tirelessly in my own corner, after a break of 20 years; not on paper but on the computer. I no longer write alone like before, but now I'm blessed to write with the One who chose and called me to this task. He directs, encourages and supports me in many ways in order for me to overcome many difficulties (especially my personal ones). Writing is not always exciting even though it's my passion. There are moments when I feel discouraged and conflicted because part of me wants to devote my life to Him, but then my flesh wonders why I have to pour all my time into this task? However, God is always near. He knows I'm weak and limited, He understands exactly what I'm going through. And in His perfect timing, He always brings me something very practical and clear as day in order for me to see the value and benefit of what I'm doing and how honored I am to be called to this. So I continue to write. And He has done that not once, but many times. God has carried me in His loving arms, and helped me overcome and realize that I'm never alone. He's been next to me silently all along.

Without Him, all the things I write would be just to ease some little sorrow or, perhaps, for my own gratification. But when I truly desire to please God, He then multiplies the fruit of my offering exceedingly.

> "I read it till 3 am!"
> "I broke down in tears..."
> "Now I know what I need to do."
> "My whole family now believes in God."
> "I'm not experienced in witnessing, I only hand it to others to read and then bring them to church..."

I am amazed and thankful to God for these testimonies. After all, I just want to say, those are not the work of my hands, but God's.

Dear friends, have you ever wanted to do something for God? That's when He's calling you. Don't let that moment pass by!

THE CREATIVE EXPLOITS OF A DOCTOR'S PEN

I sit on the Philippine Board on Books for Young People (PBBY), formerly a national section of the International Board on Books for Young People (IBBY). This 30-year-old organization comprises key players in the Philippine Children's Literature industry.

Believing that the God we serve is a god of excellence and not of mediocrity, I took part in the premier national literary contest, the Don Carlos Palanca Memorial Awards for Literature, which is considered to be the benchmark for literary achievement in the Philippines. I won prizes for both my children's stories as well as my personal essays. In 2005, after winning five Palanca first prizes, I was elevated to the Palanca Awards Hall of Fame. To date, there are only about 25 writers in the group since the award-giving body took off in 1951.

"Doc, do you write legibly?" This is how I am often teased whenever I am introduced as a doctor who writes. In the Philippines, most people equate the medical profession with poor handwriting. Probably, it is because doctors have gained the reputation of having the kind of handwriting that only pharmacists can decipher. Very often, people are just fascinated to see a medical practitioner dabbling in the world of creative writing and book development.

"If you have to choose between medicine and literature, which would it be?" a lifestyle editor once asked. She was intrigued by the idea that someone would be able to marry his passion with his profession happily. The truth of the matter is, it is difficult to serve two masters at the same time. Either you are a practicing professional or a committed artist. Not so in my case. I was gifted with a burning desire to share my thoughts through the printed page.

Balancing the Left and Right Brain

In 2003, during the search for the Ten Outstanding Young Men of the Philippines (TOYM), a nationwide program that seeks to recognize the most outstanding Filipino men under the age of 40 who had made significant contributions in various fields, a question struck me in the heart. I was one of the finalists being interviewed by the panelists. "Being a doctor and a man of letters, does it really make you outstanding?" I didn't know what to say. How was I supposed to answer the question? Fortunately, another judge in the panel quipped, "Seldom do we see a man who is able to merge the right side of his brain (the creative side) with that of the left side (the more analytical side). And he was able to produce a lot of books out of this combination." That did it!

It is a known fact that medicine requires sharp analytical skills. Writing, on the other hand, entails a high degree of creativity. To fuse these abilities would mean that the right side and the left side of the brain are in a state of equilibrium in terms of function. "Why the need to choose between Medicine and Literature when I can combine the two? Why Medicine OR Literature when it can be Medicine AND Literature?"

Juggling my professional work as a doctor and a writer is certainly not an easy thing to do. I have had to manage my time really well. In spite of my busy schedule attending to my patients, I always make time for writing. It inspires me. It gives me a reason to see better days ahead. When I'm in the clinic and an idea comes to mind, I jot it down in the small notebook that I always carry with me. My medical background and my constant engagement with my patients has provided me a rich source of stories for the books that I write.

Why Children's Literature?

Of all the literary genres, I chose to focus on children's literature. And why not? I am not the first doctor to write for children in the Philippines anyway. Dr. Jose Rizal, our National Hero, was a medical doctor too — an ophthalmologist. But he became an instrument for social reform when he wrote the two novels *Noli Me Tangere* (Touch Me Not/ The Social Cancer) and *El Filibusterismo* (The Filibuster) which helped ignite the Philippine revolution against the 300-year-old Spanish rule. The Philippines had been a colony of Spain for three centuries. Rizal's writings angered the Spaniards so much that they had him executed via a firing squad. Today, whoever said "the pen is mightier than the sword" must be thinking of the great Jose Rizal.

"If you have to choose between medicine and literature, which would it be?" a lifestyle editor once asked.

Dr. Rizal's contributions to children's literature have been influential to so many aspiring writers, myself included. He retold and illustrated a popular Filipino folktale, *The Monkey and The Tortoise*, for the enjoyment of his nephews and nieces, and he had it published in a London journal in July 1889. It then became the basis for the celebration of the National Children's Book Day in the Philippines, which happens every third Tuesday of July. Proof of Rizal's interest in children's literature was his effort to translate some of Hans Christian Andersen's classics into Tagalog. One hundred years after Rizal's death, when the nation was celebrating his centennial year of heroism in 1996, I wrote a children's book entitled *Ang Ambisyosong Istetoskop* (The Ambitious Stethoscope), telling the life of Rizal from the point of view of his stethoscope — a tribute to the first Filipino children's book author.

It has long been a personal pursuit of mine to be a writer but I never really thought I would be one. In college, I took up a pre-med course, BS Medical Technology. It eventually paved the way for me to earn a degree in Medicine. During those days, I would enter the world of microorganisms and see it as playground for creative explorations. For instance, I would attempt to simplify the life cycle of an intestinal worm through an animated storytelling session using action and humor. I gave funny names to my characters, too. Before long, my classmates would become very engrossed in what I was trying to describe. They told me that I had a very fertile imagination. Back then, being the aspiring writer that I was, I would write articles, poems, and essays not only for our school papers but for different national publications as well.

I started my career in children's literature with the biggest publisher of Christian books in the Philippines, OMF Lit, Inc., in 1993. They were then planning to come up with a concept for children's books. So they asked me if I would be willing to write a health-themed story for them. At that time, I was having my residency training in the field of Pediatrics. Sensing that God wanted me to engage in this endeavor, I began to embrace my calling as a children's literature writer. I soon came to the realization that half of the Philippine population actually comprised of school-age children. That gave an added boost to my interest in the genre.

It occurred to me that in the Philippines, particularly in the countryside, only a limited number of local children's books were available for a growing Filipino child to read. I grew up reading foreign materials, just like any other child my age, because of the lack of children's books specifically written for the Filipino audience. Hence, I resorted to reading Filipino comics which were readily available then. Most of the stories I knew were from my school textbooks and "komiks."

I was also blessed to have a great storyteller in my father who loved telling us bedtime stories. Right after dinner, we would lie down next to him to listen to his stories. With the *lub-dub, lub-dub, lub-dub* of his heart and the *kruk-kruk-swish-swash* sound of his abdomen as sound effects, I would imagine faraway lands and kingdoms, kings and queens, princes and princesses.

> With the *lub-dub, lub-dub, lub-dub* of his heart... as sound effects, I would imagine faraway lands and kingdoms, kings and queens, princes and princesses.

My grandmother also had a steady supply of *komiks* and I spent many afternoons reading with her. In fact, my first heroes and heroines were from comic magazines. I remember that I would be so immersed in the stories I read that in retelling them to my friends, I would reinvent each of their endings whenever I felt like it. I also had this nasty habit of deleting the faces of the villains in the comic illustrations, with the help of a pencil eraser. You can just imagine the horror in my grandmother's face to see her comic magazines tattered, with plenty of holes.

Taking the Plunge

I remember that I was a high-school freshman in Cabanatuan City when my father brought home copies of a Manila-based school publication. "Lui, take a look at this article written by your cousin. It's really something!" I could feel his excitement and pride as he went through the pages to show me the piece. Reading the article,

I felt that I could do it too. "So, this is how the story is written? I could give it a try." This marked the beginning of my romance with the printed word. My cousin never knew that she was the catalyst that sparked my lifelong passion for writing.

Thereafter, I represented my school in many writing contests. I always won in the inter-school competitions. My teachers would tell me that I had a way with words and that I should continue to polish it. I went on to write personal essays, poetry, and short stories while I was in medical school. Some of these were published in our national magazines and newspapers. The thought that my works were being read by a larger audience gave me a certain kind of happiness and thrill. More than the fact that writing helped me gain confidence, it saw me through the hardships of my medical studies.

I felt more accountable to the Filipino children when I fully understood God's purpose of gifting me with the ability to touch lives through writing. With the guidance of the editors and the self-help books that I'd read on writing for children, I ventured into the children's book publishing industry. The first book I wrote was about the importance of vaccinations. *May Giyera Sa Katawan ni Mark* (There's a War in Mark's Body) was printed in 1993. *How does a vaccine confer immunity? What goes on inside the body of a vaccinated child?* I was able to put all this information together into one story. Dr. Lina Diaz de Rivera, a former reading expert and professor from the University of the Philippines (UP), said that I was able to make informational books interesting with my creative approach.

I did not have any formal training on creative writing. What I did have though is a strong sense of intuition about how a certain story should be told in a particular manner. I usually assume the role of the reader when I am writing a piece. This helps me to objectively critique the piece I am writing, eliminating some biases in the process. It goes without saying that before one becomes a writer, one needs to be a reader first and foremost.

When I read any book, I always do it twice. The first time is a leisurely read. It is during my second reading that I become more critical. This is when I would study how the author handled the characterization, dialogues, narrative, the conflict, and the plot of the story. Oftentimes, I would ask: "What makes me want to read the book again? Could it be the lyricism of the text or the flair for good dialogue? How did the author construct his sentences, long or short?" Truly, I'm an intuitive writer. A lot of my writings have been born out of a gut feel for a good story.

Beyond the Horizon

To date, I have been blessed with more than 50 published children's books (some of which have been translated into Thai, Bahasa Indonesia, Japanese, and Mandarin); six self-help books which are compilations of my medical columns in weekly magazines and tabloids; and a significant number of essays anthologized in various national literary journals and school textbooks.

> Oftentimes, I would ask: "What makes me want to read the book again? Could it be the lyricism of the text or the flair for good dialogue? How did the author construct his sentences, long or short?"

Just when I thought I had done all there was to be done in writing, God allowed some of my works to be adapted into animation, opera, and musicals. *Si Duglit, Ang Dugong Makulit* (Duglit, The Pesky Blood Cell), a children's book I wrote in 1994 about the journey of a young red blood cell from someone's body to another, was chosen by the Department of Health (DOH) to be included in their list of educational materials to further the practice of voluntary blood donation in the country. Funded by the Global Fund, "Duglit..." has been adapted into an animated film utilized by the Department of Education (DepEd), Philippine Blood Center, Philippine Red Cross (PRC), and other mission-based organizations nationwide.

My children's book *Sandosenang Sapatos* (A Dozen Pairs of Shoes) was adapted into a musical presented by the resident theater company of the Cultural Center of the Philippines (CCP), the Tanghalang Pilipino. Later on, it was chosen as the Philippine entry to the 2014 International Theater Olympics in Beijing, China, and was warmly received by audiences from various nationalities. Another children's book, *Ang Pambihirang Buhok ni Raquel* (Raquel's Fantastic Hair), was made into an app by a leading publisher of children's books in the country, Adarna House, Inc. As the publishing world is now into engaging in digital platforms, the majority of my works have become digitized and converted into e-books.

Honing My Skills

Joining the Christian Writers Fellowship (CWF), which meets every last Friday of the month, was also pivotal in my journey as a Christian writer. It opened windows of opportunity for me. Moreover, it allowed me to see the impact of book writing. Before joining the CWF, I was very keen on just writing articles for magazines and newspapers. Seeing my works printed in national publications was enough for me. But a former OMF Lit editor, Ms. Jophen Baui, who used to attend the CWF monthly meetings, posted a challenge for me to consider writing books for its permanence and timelessness. She also encouraged me to focus on literary writing. "Your strength is in fiction. You have to hone it," she said.

Then the Editor-in-Chief of *Liwayway Magazine*, the country's oldest and leading Tagalog magazine in circulation, Mr. Rodolfo Salandanan, gave me an opportunity to write medical articles, regularly for the magazine. Later on, I became one of the magazine's columnists. Subsequently, he gave me another health column for *Balita*, a Tagalog news tabloid. *Balita* is *Liwayway Magazine's* sister publication. When I met the chief editor for the first time, he said, "Are you really a medical doctor? Because whenever I read your articles, I would see a writer." This was the confirmation that I had been seeking from above. Indeed, God wants me to be of service to my countrymen through my pen even while I wear my hat as a doctor.

In 2000, I launched a series of children's books called "*Mga Kuwento ni Tito Dok*" ("Stories of Uncle Doc") in partnership with OMF Lit, Inc. Each of the books centers on an ailment affecting the human body. Stories on tooth decay, dog bites, wound healing, sore eyes, common colds, fractures, intestinal parasitism, diarrhea, tonsillitis, bronchial asthma, and allergies, to name a few, all received good reviews. The series became an instant hit that was endorsed by the Department of Education (DepEd) as supplementary reading materials for elementary public schools all over the Philippines. This year will see the 20th book in the series.

The hard work that I put in to gather concepts for *Mga Kuwento ni Tito Dok (Stories of Uncle Doc)* is really like no other. I do a lot of reading and research before I am able to write the stories for each book in the health series. If I feel the need to do an actual interview, I do it without hesitation. There is no shortcut in doing things. Most especially if one is writing for the most discriminating audience of all, the children. I study as much as I can about a given topic and think of creative ways to simplify it.

> An abstract concept has to be made concrete before it is rendered into a story that child readers can easily comprehend.

An abstract concept has to be made concrete before it is rendered into a story that child readers can easily comprehend. Children are known to be concrete thinkers. It is this distinct developmental milestone feature of children that makes writing stories for them so complex. Of course, no one would want his readers to experience "indigestion" with his stories. Even something as simple as naming characters has to be done carefully. The names used, more than merely sounding good, have to mirror the personality or traits of the characters. *Duglit* is a red blood cell who is young and pesky (*paslit* and *makulit*). *Bolet* rhymes with *bulate* (worm), hence the name of the ascaris worm, *Bolet Bulate*. I gave a name *Turtoryok*

to a bacterium that infects street foods; with *"yok"* sounding a lot like "yuck."

A Rollercoaster Ride

Although it is clear that the most logical thing for a medical doctor to write about is something related to his profession, I have also written stories on socially relevant themes such as respect for the elderly, concern for the environment, adoption, coping with natural disasters, disability, children's rights.

There was a time when children's literature in the Philippines was viewed as of less importance. A senior writer once advised me to start writing more "serious literature" when I handed him copies of the children's books I had written. I resented the premise that children's literature could not be considered an authentic form of literature because in my heart I knew it's a class on its own. I may have given my characters funny names, but my writings are not any less serious.

With the passing of time, this has become a non-issue. The pain and agony of writing stories for children came to a halt in the late '90s when the landscape of children's book publishing in the Philippines dramatically improved. In recent years, among the literary genres, children's literature has grown the most.

Like anyone else, I had my share of ups and downs as a writer. Harsh comments, those that really cut to the heart, spread like wildfire following the success of my *Mga Kuwento ni Tito Dok* series. The DepEd began ordering bulk copies of my work, which reached a total of several thousand copies, to supplement the health teaching materials available for elementary students. Consequently, my integrity was questioned by a prominent writer, no less, for doing children's health books only for monetary gain. It hurt me to the core, but by God's grace, I was able to rise above it. Such moments helped me to truly understand that silence can become one's ally. Some battles are ours but, most of the time, I believe they are His.

I shrugged it all off because I knew my intentions were not only good, they were right.

Through it all I have held fast to my convictions. I was encouraged by fellow writers who dismissed the allegations as plain envy. My OMF Lit family stood by me with a reminder to never lose focus on my vision and to let my works speak for themselves. The whole time, I reminded myself of the citation that the book series received from the Manila Critics' Circle National Book Awards "...*for its popularization of the science of medicine in language and illustrations that young children can understand, for its indigenizing of universal scientific principles, and for its imaginative reconstruction of what happens in the human body.*" My journey as a doctor-writer has been a rollercoaster ride. But when I receive kind words from my child readers (and their parents), I am lost for words. They serve as a healing balm to a writer's aches.

> Seeing their faces light up as they go through the pages of my storybooks, I feel that, somehow, I have contributed something good to their childhood.

Staying the Course

Once, I had a child patient afflicted with leukemia who approached me for my book *Ang Pambihirang Buhok ni Raquel (Raquel's Fantastic Hair)*. The story is about a girl afflicted with leukemia who, instead of feeling sorry for herself for the loss of hair due to chemotherapy, wore fashionable wigs and bravely fought the battle against cancer. She asked me if she could have several copies of the book because she identified herself with the central character and she wanted each of her playmates to have a copy. The memories I have of her and other children will always be my source of strength and inspiration to continue with my crusade to write and publish books, not just for the beautiful and loved, but for the marginalized and neglected children as well.

Truly, the Lord has given me a gift of creative expression through writing and I commit myself to honing it. My Pathology professor in medical school once said that if a muscle in our body is not frequently used, it will atrophy or decrease in size. So I put my writing muscles to use to bless the children with more stories. Seeing their faces light up as they go through the pages of my storybooks, I feel that, somehow, I have contributed something good to their childhood.

I will therefore remain steadfast in my faith that God has called me to write and to heal even through the creative exploits of my pen.

THE JOURNEY OF MY PEN

ROBINSON SAMUEL GILL of Pakistan
persevered in spite of much discouragement
from the many rejections he received for
his submitted manuscripts. As he says
in his story, "In spite of rejection and
discouragement, I kept on writing." God
honored that perseverance and Robinson
is now a published author many times
over with stories and articles published by
both Christian and secular publishers. He
also serves as a Pastor, Preacher and Bible
Teacher.

How It Started

"The prince was so upset in his boat. He didn't know what to do. Suddenly, a Jinn appeared and offered him help...."

Those were the words a young boy was uttering while playing with his toys in the courtyard. His elder brother was also playing, but he was making up a story based on what the younger brother was saying. A toy boat floated in a water bucket and there were a few flowerpots and plants there in the corner of the courtyard, so both kids were pretending that it was all happening in a river by a thick forest.

On that same evening, a small, handmade, eight-page booklet came into being; a story written by the elder brother. Now both boys were anxious to have their newly written story in as many hands as possible. So their mother went along with them to a nearby photocopying shop where they had five sets of the story done. Four A4-sized sheets of paper were printed on both sides. After folding the sheets in half, a booklet of seven written pages along with the black-and-white title page drawn by the elder brother was ready to be sold! The first person to buy that booklet was the owner of that photocopying shop. The handmade booklet containing the short story was greatly appreciated by family members and friends.

That was the point in my life when I realized that I had the talent of writing. It was more than 25 years ago when I was playing with my younger brother Solomon, but my pen is still journeying on. My mother, Iris Gill, played a vital role in encouraging me from that point on. My hobbies were playing music, sketching, reading and pen friendship. I had lots of Christian pen friends to whom I frequently wrote letters. Reading Christian storybooks published by the Christian publishing house known as *Masihi Isha'at Khana* (MIK) was also one of my favorite hobbies. I assume I inherited this habit from my paternal grandfather, William Gill. My father remembers seeing his dad sleeping with a book on his chest. He was so fond of reading Christian books because he was a preacher, teacher, pastor, and a host of a Christian Radio program. My mother is also an avid reader. In my childhood, my favorite writer was *Baji Nasreen*. I always loved reading her short stories (published by MIK) which were packaged in small booklets with attractive and colorful covers.

A Time of Blissful Ignorance

In 1993, when I read a story book called *Khatarnak Mohem* (Dangerous Adventure) written by Elizabeth Greig and published by MIK, I was so inspired that I decided to write one of my own. At that time I had completed my high school education. I used to sit every evening and regularly write four or five pages. After writing and completing the final manuscript for *The Punishment of Disobedience*, I posted it to MIK assuming that the next storybook published by them would be mine. For me, this was the stage of 'blissful ignorance' that Dianne Doubtfire wrote about in her book *Creative Writing*. In my mind, I imagined myself being a great help to MIK by writing a new story every month. They would then have plenty of storybooks to publish. I had read almost all the MIK story books written for my age group at that time and I kept on waiting for more to come soon. I began to think of myself as a prolific writer, even though nothing had been published yet!

> I began to think of myself as a prolific writer, even though nothing had been published yet!

A Time of Discouragement

After some time, I received a very encouraging letter from Mr. Peter Calvin, one of the editors of MIK, who is presently the General Manager. This letter was written in his own handwriting. That was a great encouragement for me. In the letter he advised me to begin with short stories and also to attend the upcoming Christian Writers' Workshop that was to be run by MIK. For various reasons, I was not able to attend the workshop that same year, but in the meantime I wrote a short story and sent it to Mr. Peter Calvin. He sent back the edited story with another very encouraging letter and some instructions. He advised me to send it to a Christian magazine called *Rahbar*.

Our family was already receiving that magazine which was published eight times a year. Articles written by my father, Samuel Gill, were already being published in that magazine. So I sent my story to *Rahbar* and soon received a letter from Mr. Maqbool Gill, the editor at the time, saying that my story had been accepted and would be published soon. Immediately, my pen started flowing again, like an endless spring. However, the time of discouragement continued, as none of my subsequent stories were ever published in *Rahbar* magazine for almost a year. I joined the Christian Writers' Workshop held by the *Rahbar* Magazine staff in 1994 and met some Christian writers and writers-to-be. That was when I came to the realization that I was not a writer — that it was not as easy as I thought.

> "A writer actually persuades a person to listen to him (through his pen) while he himself is not present with that person."

So I thought, why on earth would anyone want to read my stuff! However, soon after the workshop, I was encouraged to see one of my stories, which I had written during the Writers' Workshop, published in their magazine. And so the journey of my rusty pen started once again.

In 1995, I sent a story to *Rahbar* which, like many others, was rejected. With some discouragement and a sense of rejection, I edited and refined the story according to the guidelines given to me by one of the *Rahbar* staff. However, rather than sending it back to *Rahbar*, I sent it to a well-known non-Christian children's and youth magazine called *Nonehal*. To my amazement, the story was published after two months and I received a complimentary copy plus an honorarium. I was terribly excited because that important magazine was first published in 1953. It was a magazine with a very large circulation. It was such an honor for me to see a magazine in every bookshop with my story in it. It was like a turbo for the journey of my pen. However, for the next year or so, none of my subsequent stories was accepted by *Nonehal*.

Coping With Rejection

In a writer's life, rejections are commonplace in the beginning. However, if you receive the rejections along with instructions and advice about what you have written, you can learn a lot. This rejection phase actually turned into a great learning period for me. But the secret behind the success is to keep on writing. Many a times when my submissions were rejected, I would feel so disappointed that I'd even forgot where I had put my favorite pen! However, the journey didn't cease. After I saw my published stories in *Rahbar* or *Nonehal*, I started writing again. On average, for every one of my stories published, I would write five more as a result of the encouragement and inspiration received.

> This rejection phase actually turned into a great learning period for me.

Now I often say that even if I were in prison or alone on an island, I'd need only a pen and notebook to write in and I would survive. Writing is my passion, my hobby, the integral part of my life. I make entries in my journal regularly. I always have a pocket-sized notebook with me to take notes and write down observations or to save the new ideas that come to mind. But I did not reach this stage suddenly or just by chance. It involved lots of encouragement as well as rejection and discouragement. Many people have played a vital role in the journey of my pen.

In spite of rejection and discouragement, I kept on writing. The rejected story from *Rahbar* opened the door for me into a non-Christian children's magazine, *Nonehal*. Then multiple rejections from *Nonehal* opened other new avenues for me. As I began to send my rejected stories with some minor changes and improvements to another magazine, they started to publish them on a regular basis. That was a great encouragement for me. I began to see improvements in my writing as a result of also attending the writers' workshops regularly. In one magazine, *Fiction*, my submission won the prize for the best story. The same thing happened three times consecutively. I began to receive good comments and phone calls from the readers, which was also a source of great encouragement.

In the writers' workshops held by *Rahbar* and MIK, we were encouraged to read secular writers too. So I began to focus on that. I read well-known Pakistani as well as foreign writers who helped me immensely to improve my writing skill and develop my writing style.

About ten years ago, I was walking with one of my uncles, Dr. William George, who has since returned to the Lord (in 2013). After hearing about my published stories, he said, "Keep saving them. One day they may be published in book form."

I asked myself, *"Why on earth would any publisher want to publish my already published material?"* But that very thing happened in 2011. When MIK saw my published stories, they offered to publish them in book form. I remember I sent my first story to MIK in 1993. Since then, I had never tried again. After such a long journey, my pen is now so much more skillful. Finally, after 18 years, my first storybook was published by MIK and they now publish my writings on a regular basis. So far, more than 100 of my stories have been published in different magazines.

At the age of ten, I said that I would become a preacher as my grandfather and father both served the Lord through this ministry. I accepted the Lord Jesus Christ in 1992 at the age of 16. While in college, I chose subjects that would be helpful for my further studies in a Bible Seminary. By God's grace, after receiving my Bachelor of Divinity Degree with Honors from Spurgeon's College London, I am now serving as a Pastor, Preacher, and a Bible Teacher.

I thank God for giving me this wonderful ability to write. Now I understand why God has gifted me with this skill. I believe that it is my responsibility, duty, as well as divine calling to keep writing. It is so vital for me. I praise God that I have access to various non-Christian magazines through my pen. Many times, I have written stories with some Biblical message or based on a biblical verse or even on Jesus' parables. I understand that Jesus has called us to be the salt of this earth. Through my writings, my influence is like salt in this society.

> I believe that it is my responsibility, duty, as well as divine calling to keep writing. It is so vital for me.

Recently, I met the editor of a youth magazine and he said, *"We like your writing so much. I am so confident about your writing that often I don't even read or edit your stories. I just put them in the magazine and later read them in published form."* That was indeed a great compliment for me. Presently, I'm writing in various Christian as well as non-Christian magazines like *Emmanuel Youth Magazine (EYMag), Nia Tadeeb, Anokhi Kahanian, Arxang, Taleem-O-Tarbiat* and *Saathee*.

I also owe a great deal to my wife Kiran for her constant encouragement and for allowing me to carry on this valuable task of writing in addition to my ministry as a pastor. She is usually the first reader of my initial manuscript. She not only encourages me, but she is my valued critic as well.

My Inspiration

I believe that a true and creative writer cannot write without inspiration. There are many factors that could inspire a writer to pick up his pen and express his feelings. Usually, my inspirations come out in the form of a story as that is the most fascinating and appealing genre for me. I also love writing travelogues as we learn a lot through traveling. The lessons learnt make the travelogue richer and more effective. Traveling to an interesting new place could inspire me to write. An interesting book or some biblical truth would inspire me to write a story.

Clouds, rain, beautiful landscapes, pleasant weather are fascinating triggers for me to start writing something. However a bitter experience, a frustration, or some kind of tension could also cause me to write. And that's where a writer gets greatest satisfaction because his pen provides him with catharsis too.

The encouragement from readers also inspires me to write more. I appreciate my sister Ruby Naeem and sister-in-law, Anita Solomon who are always the first to read and praise my writings.

In conclusion, I would say that starting a story or a piece of writing is the hardest job. However, once you start, you will find enjoyment and, at the end, an amazing satisfaction when you see your work being published.

I would like to encourage new writers to write, write and write, because writing is the most satisfying and comforting act one can do.

I praise and thank God that the journey of my pen is still going on well and I will continue this journey to the end of my days.

MY JOURNEY THROUGH THE SCRIPTS OF LIFE

GEORGE KOSHY has a degree in Chemistry and a postgraduate degree in Journalism and Mass Communication. He has authored 24 books and more than 70 christian hymns. He freelances for various christian TV channels and is currently the Editorial Director for Sathgamaya Media Foundation who publish in print, audio, visual and digital media in 15 Indian languages. He has received three major literary awards. He is married to Sheena and they have two children, Paul and Veda.

There was a slight drizzle as I walked from school that evening. But I was determined to open my shop and sell my wares even in the rain. I conducted my business under the shade of a coffee bean tree in our backyard and my customers were patrons who dropped by every day for a friendly chat and some transactions. One of these patrons was my mother who never failed to buy some potatoes and onions that I had modelled from clay, or drumsticks that had been fashioned from twigs. To my five-year-old eyes, everything in the yard could be magically transformed into treasured trinkets that I would then proudly display in my shop and sell, mostly to my family members.

That evening was no different. I opened my "shop" and my mother arrived to make her "purchases." As she negotiated the price with me, one of our neighbours came by to chat with her. Their conversation soon turned to domestic concerns and I could not understand much of what they said. So I busied myself with display arrangements. But suddenly, one of mom's statements leapt out from their conversation and remained stuck in my mind. What she said was, "the elephant finds the log burdensome but an ant finds a grain burdensome." This sentence kept playing in my head and soon I closed the shop and ran home. Later, as I prepared for bed, I kept mumbling mom's statement to myself. Soon, I fell asleep.

The next morning, I started from where I had left off the previous night with the elephant and the ant. By now I had attached a tune to the sentence. I went about getting ready for school and mom, a school teacher, was also getting ready for work. We went to the same school, she to teach and I to study. My ditty now progressed into two more sentences. Unexpectedly I sang, "The elephant finds the log burdensome, the ant finds the grain burdensome, but I find nothing burdensome, because Jesus took my burdens away." Mom instantly turned around and asked, "What did you just sing?" I froze. What had I done? Was it blasphemy to put elephants, ants, and Jesus together into four lines? Would mom punish me? Afraid of the consequences, I quipped, "Nothing ma!" But she persisted. "Sing that again," she said. Anticipating a whack from her, I sang my lines again. Mom's eyes sparkled and, with a beaming smile, she hugged me and kissed me. "That's wonderful!" she exclaimed. "Sing it once more, please!" She made me sing the little chorus many more times. And before we left home, she called my older sister and asked her to write the lines in a book so that we would not forget it. (I was just beginning to read and write). "You must do this again," she encouraged, "and make sure you sing it out to me."

> "The elephant
> finds the log
> burdensome,
> the ant finds
> the grain
> burdensome, but
> I find nothing
> burdensome,
> because Jesus
> took my burdens
> away."

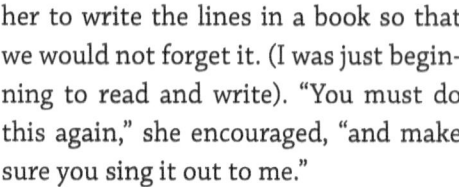

I was over the moon. I could barely recognize alphabets but I was already declared a writer. And both my older sisters treated their little writer baby brother with much affection and encouragement. Had it not been for my mom's keen ears and the support of all my family members, my literary career would have begun and ended in oblivion with that four-line amateur song. It was their unconditional love and support that formed the foundation of my literary exploits.

The World of Books

I remember someone saying that "a good reader makes a good writer." So I began to read any printed material that I could find. The most common was the daily newspaper but most of the material was unappealing to my mind. My eyes then wandered over to the comic strips with Mandrake the Magician and Phantom. I eagerly awaited each day's copy to read about my heroes. As I grew older dad began to buy books for me and I was gifted books for every special occasion, be it birthdays or holidays. And I couldn't have been happier. My library now holds over 6,000 books.

New words and phrases excited me and each time I came across one, I would write it in my notebook, then look for opportunities to use them on my own. Thus my vocabulary grew immensely. This habit has stuck with me all these years and has helped me with my writing.

A Poetic Beginning

I loved the language classes at school. During these sessions the teacher would read us poetry in Malayalam (my mother tongue) and tell us about the poets and their lives and experiences. I was enthralled by the stories and also loved to learn about their styles and expressions. My mind bent heavily towards all things poetic and I began to write—compulsively and very often aimlessly. During those early days, I composed innumerable rhymes and poems.

Another force that drove me towards poetry was the writings of Mahakavi (Poet Laureate) K. V. Simon. He was one of the pioneers of the Brethren Movement in Kerala, South India, and his writings, speeches, hymns, and poetry exerted a great influence over that generation. The Brethren church that I attended used many of his songs during the worship services. His classical musical compositions continued to amaze me. It was K.V. Simon's biography, which included his writings, that introduced me to the serious nature of poetry and how this medium could be used to learn and to teach biblical truths.

Thus I began to adapt new styles to my writing. One of my first pieces was a poem based on the parable of the wise and foolish builders in Matthew 7:24-27. Though I was proud of my work, in retrospect, I don't think that piece of writing could even be termed as good literature. However, one of the editors of our church publication printed my poem to encourage the writer in me and thus, for the first time, my name appeared in print. I was 11 years old then.

This incident gave me much confidence and I sent one of my poems to a secular children's magazine. But I had very little hope that they would ever print my material. Two weeks later, however, my uncertainties were quashed. The postman arrived with a copy of the children's magazine and a paycheck of 35 rupees (50 cents) with my name on it. In my little world, I had arrived. At least, that's what my friends thought. They were overjoyed to read my poem in the magazine and pestered me for a treat. My first earnings as a writer were only enough to buy a few candies for my friends. But from that day on, they encouraged me wholeheartedly, partly in anticipation of another round of candy treats!

A Reality Check

As I grew older, my poetry began to mature too and I began sending it to various magazines in the hope of publishing them. One of the more widely read weekly magazines accepted my poem and printed it. The week it was published, I happened to undertake a bus journey. Coincidentally, I found my co-passenger reading a copy of the very same magazine. My joy knew no bounds and my ego was exploding with excitement. He was a few pages away from my poem. And I hoped to introduce myself to the reader when he reached the page. So I steadied my collar, adjusted my sleeves, ran my fingers through my hair, and readied myself for the big presentation.

> My excitement and ego plummeted and were reduced to ashes. I had just received the dreaded live "rejection slip" and it was painful.

The man read the cover story, glanced through the smaller features and articles and then arrived at the page with my poem. He peeked into the page for a split second and then turned to the next article. My excitement and ego plummeted and were reduced to ashes. I had just received the dreaded live "rejection slip" and it was painful. However, this was the reality check that I desperately needed at that time. I had met a different kind of a reader — a representative of the masses that did not think that poetry was worth their time. That bumpy bus ride taught me that if I continued with poetry, I would be able to communicate only with a select few of the population. I got off the bus with a determination to try other genres as well.

A Lost Trophy

My tryst with poetry was far from over. My poems competed at both the school and district levels. I secured the first place during one of these competitions and won a foot-long trophy. As I exited the stage with my prize, the event organizer approached me and said, "We need to emboss the sponsor's name on the trophy. So please return it. I'll deliver it to your school tomorrow." But that tomorrow never came. The trophy that brought me my first public recognition is probably languishing in some forgotten corner of a dusty workshop.

A Detour

With school behind me, it was time for career choices. Every cell in my being was driving me towards a career in language, literature, writing, journalism, and mass communication. But I also had to think logically and practically about my future. Though a career in writing would be ideal with my skill and talents, it would never allow me financial security or independence. (Writers are supposed to be extraordinary creatures who feed on high thinking and lofty ideas. Society at large assumes that the basic necessities of food, shelter, clothing, salary, etc., are not applicable to this section of humanity.) Therefore, I decided to try my luck at studying medicine. I made all the preliminary arrangements and also began to study for the entrance examinations. Fortunately for thousands of patients, I did not get the required number of points to pursue a degree in medical science. The next option was to take a course in pharmacology to be a chemist. That door was shut too.

The Prodigal Returns

The only option that remained was to say goodbye to lucrative job prospects and follow my heart and gut and mind and every cell in my body, and choose a career in journalism. Like a prodigal I returned to the house of poetry, comics, journalism, writing, and editing. My days of wandering in foreign career paths were over and I finally signed up for a post-graduate course in journalism and mass communication. I was finally on the path that God had prepared for me.

I felt at home. Along with the course, I also secured an internship with a newspaper and worked as a sub-editor.

On completion of the course, I landed a job at one of the reputed newspapers in India with the highest number of publications. To my delight, I was placed in charge of the comics and story section. I was now closer than ever to my childhood comic strip heroes. Moreover, I was getting paid for doing something that I so loved. This was an unbelievable situation for me. Thus far, I had nothing to complain. I had a job that I loved and was paid quite well. But somewhere in the depth of my heart was a sense of restlessness and dissatisfaction. But I ignored it and spent all my energy doing my job. Till God dramatically crossed my path.

A Message in a Bus

One evening after work, I boarded a bus for home and, as I sat down, I noticed a book lying on the next seat. Out of plain curiosity I picked it up and discovered that it was a Bible. I flipped through the pages and the verse in I Timothy 4:7 jumped off the page. *"But have nothing to do with worldly fables fit only for old women. On the other hand, discipline yourself for the purpose of Godliness."* The verse read like my job description. It was a direct invitation for me to quit wasting my time with "worldly fables fit only for old women" and focus on life-giving words. My days at the brook of Kerith, feeding on what the raven brought, were over. I quit my job and dedicated my life to the literature ministry.

> My days of wandering in foreign career paths were over and I finally signed up for a post-graduate course in journalism and mass communication.

Soon I joined one of the premier Christian publishing houses in India, Gospel Literature Service, and began another phase of my career. The training and exposure that I had received in the secular field proved useful as I moved into this new field. My heart was firmly set on producing biblical literature for children.

Literature for Kids

At that time, though 38 percent of the Indian population was under 18, the percentage of Christian literature produced for them was a measly 0.6 percent. These numbers haunted me. The Lord gave me a new and urgent mandate—to produce biblical literature for children, especially in vernacular languages. Since the Malayalam language was my forte, I plunged into producing books, magazines, stories, songs, and videos for children.

My task was far from over. If producing literature and audio-video material was the first part of the challenge, the next part was to take it to the homes, hands, and hearts of the target audience. Parents of that era happily bought clothes, toys, and various other treats for their children. But books were not one of them. So my first job was to break through the existing social mindset and create a need for the product. Thus with the help of various organizations, we arranged family conferences where we conducted sessions on the need for creating a reading habit in children and also instilling biblical values in them. Another strategy was to conduct book release functions during conventions and other Christian gatherings. We also began to communicate directly with the children. We conducted exclusive children's meetings with puppet shows, games, story time, etc., and placed book stalls in every gathering.

In 1992 there was a major turning point in my life when I met Larry Brook, a trainer at the Chicago-based (now in Colorado Springs) Cook Communications Ministries International (CCMI). He suggested that I would benefit much from the International Christian Publishing Institute (ICPI) at CCMI and invited me to join. It was an exclusive training session on Children's psychology and literature. This training opened my eyes to the manifold opportunities and possibilities that could be utilized in children's ministry. I felt like Alice in a publishing wonderland! God challenged me when I was at ICPI. And I returned with renewed vigor. First on my list of priorities was a Bible for Children in Malayalam.

The Bible that the Rats Ravaged

In 1840 the first Indian-language Bible was published in India. Over 150 years later, though 18 percent of India's 1 billion people are children and teens, no one had yet to produce a children's Bible in an Indian language.

When I returned after the training at ICPI, I brought back several versions of the English-language Bible for children with the hope that one day I would be able to produce a similar product. With the Bibles stacked one on top of the other on a table, I began to pray. Many questions flooded my mind. Even if I were to prepare the manuscript, who would publish it? Who would draw the pictures? Who would market it? I brooded day after day.

Parents of that era happily bought clothes, toys, and various other treats for their children. But books were not one of them.

Not long afterwards, my prayers were answered. God opened a door without much delay. As it turned out, the Bible Society of India (BSI) was looking for an editor to develop a children's Bible for the Indian market. I gladly took on the challenge.

Realizing the great need for such a Bible, I asked some friends to help me write the text. The manuscript was finished in three years. However, because of some theological and other practical problems, the project was shelved. The handwritten manuscript was packed and kept in a wooden cupboard.

Years later, BSI decided to revive the project and they contacted me. I eagerly went to get the manuscript. To my horror, all that was left were a few shreds of paper and some dust. I could not believe my eyes.

Three years' work was gone. The manuscript had provided a sumptuous feast for a few mice.

I then embarked on a marathon race. Nights and holidays were completely dedicated to this project. In just 18 months, a new manuscript was ready. BSI managed to get the copyright to some great pictures using their International contacts.

While waiting for the text to be completed, BSI began to promote the Bible. A full-color brochure was prepared. Endorsements from major church leaders were sought. Christian magazines featured interviews with me and information on the product.

At last, the release of the Children's Bible took place at a grand event, with extensive media coverage. It was held at a renowned school, and Bible-based plays and programs were staged. Special discounts were offered. To the non-Christian market, it was promoted as an ideal collection of stories to help children improve their values. BSI found staff at various Christian schools to promote and sell the product.

In the state of Kerala , Kids Bible festivals were held in three key towns to promote the Bible. The fonts used in the banner, fliers, and other publicity materials for the festivals matched those of the Bible.

The multi-layered promotion helped create the impression that the Bible was the ideal gift for any child. Within the first year, 20,000 copies had been sold. Reprints of the first children's Bible still continue in full swing.

Although mice first enjoyed the manuscript, today thousands of children find it sweeter than honey.

Now it is available in several Indian languages. Videos and music albums of the Bible stories were also produced. We have a mammoth challenge in reaching Indian children and young people for Christ. This was a good beginning.

The Bible in Pictures was primarily targeted at eight- to twelve-year-olds. The Bible Society published it and were amazed at the overwhelming response it received. Soon they commissioned me to produce a Bible in Pictures for the younger age groups as well.

The next major task was to produce a book that would familiarize young adults and new believers with basic Bible doctrines. Out of this need came the book *Face to Face with God* which explained 52 fundamentals of the Christian faith. Produced by Campus Crusade for Christ, this title has now been translated into ten languages and, in the coming days, they hope to translate it into 50 languages.

> I felt like a Lilliputian among these literary giants and, during that conference, my feet and ego touched the ground of reality.

When I was approached with an offer to anchor a Christian television program, I accepted it and hoped that the added visibility and publicity that it provided would benefit my books. This weekly show ran for five years and later I did many television shows and programs for kids.

Meanwhile, I turned my attention to writing specialized tracts and booklets for children. Some of it included *Happy Birthday* published by World Vision International, and also the Malayalam version of the *Manga Messiah*, which were both well received. Moreover, I was a regular contributing writer for *Imprint*, by David C. Cook, and also *Interlit*, their magazine for writers. My literary career seemed to be soaring and unfortunately so did my pride.

A New Outlook

I first learned about Media Associates International (MAI) in 1996, when I happened to see an MAI newsletter. I had never come across a similar ministry before that. I hoped to attend the LittWorld Conference someday. But I felt that for an ordinary writer from India, it was only a dream. But God is interested in dreamers. I received a scholarship and was able to attend LittWorld in 2002 in the Philippines with visionaries from 36 other nations. It was definitely an eye-opener to me.

It was with slight hints of megalomania that I arrived in the Philippines for the LittWorld Conference. Here, I met writers and trainers who were truly amazing, in every sense of the word. They were not only fine, committed Christians who were passionate about spreading the Word, but also had achieved much more, with minuscule resources. Indeed, much more than I had ever dreamed of. Then it dawned on me that I was not worthy to even touch the shoelace of any of these men and women, let alone be called a writer. I felt like a Lilliputian among these literary giants and, during that conference, my feet and ego touched the ground of reality.

This conference taught me the need for professionalism in ministry. Though the content of our products surpasses all other worldly publications in depth and meaning, I learnt about the need for fine-tuning our product to appeal to the secular market; about the need for systems, planning, page layout, cover design, and marketing strategies. And most importantly, the need for humility as a writer.

I spent most of my time there in bookshops, learning and absorbing everything around me. The finest lessons came from the sessions and lives of John Maust, Ramon Rocha, Richard Crespo, Dan Elliott, Nate Butler, Lawrence Darmani, and many others whose names escape my memory now. However, the lessons and the encouragement they imparted are fresh in my mind after all these years. Subsequently, I was invited to the LittWorld in 2004, but this time as a plenary speaker on Children's Publishing. MAI also trained me as a trainer.

I came back from the Philippines with a determination to train and encourage young writers. I learnt that my duty as a writer included training the next generation to carry on the work. God honored this decision and gave me an opportunity to serve as a trustee on the board of MAI-Asia. In those five years, I had the privilege of training budding writers in the Philippines, Nairobi, Brazil, Sri Lanka, Bahrain, Doha, and various parts of India. These workshops gave me the chance to make many friends with a new generation of writers and I cherish these relationships that we have been able to establish. I am indebted to MAI for guiding me towards greater heights as a writer and trainer. Those days are truly unforgettable.

Confronting a Secular Market

As my horizons widened, I was convinced that biblical literature could not be limited to a Christian audience. My next passion was to take Bible-based literature to the secular market. But I did not have a strategy to accomplish this task. God sent me the answers during the LittWorld Conference in Sao Paulo. I presented my dilemma to the trainers and after the brainstorming session, we came to the conclusion that it would be best to introduce Christian literature during popular Christian occasions and festivals like Christmas and Easter. They encouraged me to think of topics that would appeal to a secular audience.

> Writing is never a lucrative job. Sometimes, I look at my friends in other professions and feel a tinge of envy at the luxuries they enjoy because of their jobs.

This discussion opened my mind to various possibilities. Suddenly I saw a wide range of opportunities that I could utilize to convey biblical values. Topics ranging from family, to children, to traditional devotionals, etc., were used and I wrote over 70 articles for secular newspapers and journals. In December 2013, from the beginning of the month till Christmas day, one of the renowned secular newspapers of India published a series of articles that I contributed about classic Christmas books. Famous Christmas stamps of the world formed another series of articles.

Visits to the Holy Land

I have visited Israel, Palestine, Jordan, and the neighboring areas 20 times and these trips enabled me to write various features and books about the Holy Land. One of the first articles was about Christmas celebrations in Bethlehem, and it was published by a leading newspaper. A well-known publishing house in Kerala noticed this article and asked me to produce a coffee-table book about the Holy Land. Every year, over 15,000 people from India visit the Holy Land and the publishing company saw this as a feasible niche product. Moreover, a travel agency which operates tours to the Holy Land, bought 1000 copies to use as their promotional material. Since the book was written in the form of a novel, it clearly conveyed the Gospel and various biblical values and principles.

Bible Museum

On the top floor of my house is a Bible Museum which contains various artefacts from the Holy Land. Visitors to this Museum can avail themselves of a guided tour through the history of the Bible and Bible lands. They will then be encouraged to spend time at the adjoining bookshop-cum-library. This arrangement has thus attracted many people to books and reading.

Combating Secular Publications

Most of my inspiration for my writing has been from my surroundings. Thus when the movie on the DaVinci Code was released, many Christians did not know what to make of it. Many missionaries also found it difficult to effectively answer the arguments that people raised about the Jesus of the movie. The need of the hour was to write about the uniqueness of Christ. Thus came the book, *DaVinci Code: Mysteries Decoded*. This was published by a secular publisher and they sold 2,000 copies within two months.

The famous Harry Potter series had taken the world by storm and these stories were running amok among children of my state too. Most parents realized that these books which glorified witchcraft were detrimental to young minds but did not know how to make children understand these values. Out of this dilemma arose the next book, *Harry Potter: Satan's Bait.*

Yet another source of inspiration came from a famous traditional dirge. When a Christian in Kerala dies, the body is usually kept in a morgue for a couple of days to give the family time to make funeral arrangements. On the day of the funeral, a band accompanies the body from the morgue to the home of the deceased. The vehicle with the band will have a loud speaker attached to it blaring various Christian hymns of hope and comfort. But every funeral procession, regardless of the denomination, will have the classic dirge, *"In the chariot of time, I journey towards heavenly shores."* This song can be heard at least once a day in our hometown and people of all religions are familiar with it.

This Malayalam song was written by a German missionary, who came to India centuries ago, learnt Malayalam and, among many other things, gifted this song for the people of Kerala to sing during their time of grief and loss. This prompted me to write his biography and it was received well by people across all faiths.

These experiences taught me that inspiration and opportunity are all around us. We merely need to keeps our eyes and minds open.

A Dream Project

It has been my dream to write a book based on the life of Christ. I am aware of the ocean of books available on this subject but I wanted to approach and present this topic in a slightly different manner. At the time of writing, I am confident that the book that has been conceived in my mind will be unique in the Malayalam language. I began this project ten years ago and I am sure that it will take a few more years to complete this task.

Recently, I had the opportunity to write the story of an ex-communist who became a follower of Christ. This story has now been turned into a film. The book about the Holy Land will also soon be turned into a film. Some of my books are now available in digital format on my personal website www.unclegk.in. These new media have enabled me to reach more readers and viewers.

The Challenges

One of the greatest challenges I now face are time constraints. Sometimes I am unable to channel my undivided attention to the project at hand. Since I am compelled to be a part of other endeavors, my writing assignments suffer in the bargain. As a result, I am tempted to compromise on the quality of my work. Since this guilt is too heavy, I often extend the deadlines so that the content will not suffer. Experience has taught me the need to impose strict deadlines on myself and sometimes fight all odds to uphold them.

Another challenge that most independent writers face is the task of marketing their books. This problem has no quick-fix solution. It is an uphill task. However, I have noticed that niche publications are easier to market. For example, when the Pentecostal group of churches was creating a set of evangelistic strategies, I told them about the need for creating appropriate literature for their mission fields. To aid them in the ministry, I produced literature for them and over three *lakh* (3,00,000) copies of this publication were distributed within a year.

Another niche publication was the one entitled *Happy Independence Day*, which is an evangelistic tool that is specially meant to be given on August 15, the day India celebrates her independence. Over one *lakh* copies (1,00,000) of this booklet were distributed on one day.

Another booklet that is targetted at a young audience in search of success is *You Too Can Win*. Fourteen million of these booklets have been distributed in various places and have touched many lives. Several thousand evangelists are disseminating it across India. The following is just one of many stories that are worth more than a hundred awards and laurels.

The Answer Is Blowing in the Wind

This is the true story of Thomas (name changed) who came to know the Lord after reading this booklet.

> *He slumped in the corner of a busy bus station in Kerala, India, and wondered how to end his miserable life. He had fallen into financial difficulties the last few years, and his debts were piling up monstrously. Moneylenders had begun harassing his wife and children too. Thomas saw only darkness ahead. He wondered whether he should hang himself, drink poison, or throw himself in front of a train.*
>
> *The wind began to blow fiercely. Candy wrappers, ticket stubs and other bits swirled around Thomas's legs. He was too preoccupied to brush them away. Then another gust blew away the papers except for a small booklet. Absentmindedly, Thomas picked it up and began to read.*
>
> *Titled* You Too Can Win, *the booklet described the love, peace and hope that Jesus Christ offers. A local pastor had distributed the booklet earlier that day. Some people had accepted it, while others had thrown it away. One of the discarded copies had clung to Thomas's leg.*
>
> *Thomas hungrily absorbed every word and committed his life to Christ in that noisy bus station. He also contacted the pastor, using the information in the leaflet, and today Thomas is a happy member of God's family.*

Though the challenges are many, the rewards are immense too. A writer can rest with the assurance that someone he has never met will be reading his book. Or that someone will find Jesus Christ in the pages of his book. The best rewards come in the form of reader responses. No award or recognition can match these perks.

Writing is never a lucrative job. Sometimes, I look at my friends in other professions and feel a tinge of envy at the luxuries they enjoy because of their jobs. But I quickly shake myself out of that and focus on the immense task that lies ahead of me. Faithful is the One who has called me and there is nothing more luxurious than being an obedient tool in His hands. I did not choose to become a writer. Rather, the Lord forcefully gave me His pen and told me to be His "ready writer." Hence I shall "address my verses to the King." Always.

MY GOD-GIVEN DESTINY

EVA KRISTIAMAN of Indonesia graduated in 1993 with a Bachelor's Degree in Theology from Duta Wacana Christian University. She then started devoting her time and passion to writing and publishing materials that show the love of God to man, and the promise of eternal salvation to those who hold on to Him. She subsequently co-founded and became the Director of Salt and Light of the World Publishing House. Currently living in Sydney, Australia, Eva is also involved in the work of Global Recordings Network Australia.

"If you could choose the job you would most like to do, what would that be?" Rose, Human Resources Director of an international company, asked me warmly. "To be a writer," I replied. I smiled and waited for her response.

"Oh, wow, that's really interesting and surprising. What a change from the children's ministry you have been involved in for more than 30 years." Her beautiful smile comforted me.

"Yes, I know...," I replied with a laugh.

More than it being the best job or career that I would want to have, I know that it is my God-given destiny. This was something I had found out a few weeks before my conversation with Rose! Writing this chapter has made me ponder afresh about my passion.

Praying is very important for me as a Christian writer, and I always ask my close friends to pray for me and for my writing. God is the source of the inspiration I need for my writing. He helps me to see, to feel, to imagine, and to remember all the memories and experiences I have had. He gives me ideas, insights, and the right words for my writing. The more I get stuck, the more I need Him. Even in the writing of this piece, I encountered writer's block. No one but God could help me.

The Solid Foundation

I had never dreamt of becoming an author. I was born in the scenic small town of Batu. About 800 meters above sea level, it is surrounded by majestic mountains. A tourist destination, it is 18 kilometers from a bigger city, Malang, in East Java, Indonesia.

The Author of my life had placed me in a small, simple, Christian family that loves God. Reading the Bible was a must and, usually, five to ten minutes prior to dinner we would sing a hymn, read the Indonesian translation of the daily devotional *The Upper Room*, and pray.

I remember I was always so tempted to grab the newspaper when it came because I couldn't wait to read the next installment of the story series at the bottom of page 3. Weekends were especially fun because of the stories and comics for children and youth in the two middle pages of the newspaper. I would also wait for the best weekly children's magazine in the '60s – '70s, *Si Kuncung*,[1] and read all 16 pages of it the day it arrived.

Another occasion I would await with eager anticipation was the moment my Mom and my elder brother came home from book shopping. They were tasked with buying books for the Sunday School library of our small church. My brother organized the books and I was the one who read them all. *Treasures of the Snow*, *The Chronicles of Narnia*, *The Pilgrims Progress*, and *The Jungle Doctor* were some of the many classics translated into Indonesian. I became familiar with names like David Livingstone, Corrie Ten Boom, and John Sung because I loved reading their biographies. There were also many very good books for children, written by Indonesian Christian writers and published by Indonesian Christian publishing houses. My Mom would often have to call me several times, before I could stop reading and put down the book. I especially liked the Danny Orlis novel series for its suspense.

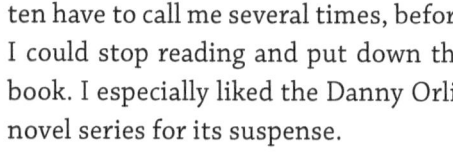

Although no one knew that the poem that was chosen to be read was mine, it didn't matter!

I also loved listening to stories from "the green book." This was the New Testament and Old Testament Bible Stories book, with its green hard cover, written by Anne de Vries. My Mom had been reading the stories to me from the time I was a baby until I could read the big book myself. Having a captivating storyteller like my Mom, who was also a very diligent Sunday School teacher, is one of God's wonderful blessings I've always been thankful for.

---

[1] *Si Kuncung* is the tuft of hair from the crown to the forehead.

God's truth and values, together with the very good Indonesian language used in those stories, books, newspaper, and magazine have all given me a solid foundation to be the kind of storyteller and writer that God has called me to be.

The Dancing Feeling

"Merdeka!" A lady's voice boldly started reading word by word the "17th August 1945" poem. It was the 29th Indonesian Independence Day ceremony at the center of my hometown, and as she clearly and beautifully read the poem, we were led to ponder afresh the meaning of the sacrifices made for our freedom.

The flames of the bamboo torches we brought were dancing quietly in the dusk, yet there was another feeling dancing merrily in my heart. *Oh my, I recognize that poem! It's mine! I had written it for the Inter-Junior-High-School Independence Day competition in my town. And it's been chosen!* When I heard her read the heroic last word of the poem powerfully and confidently, "Merdeka!", my heart pounded in response, *"Merdeka!" Yes, Freedom!"*

Oh, that is the dancing feeling of getting published! Although no one knew that the poem that was chosen to be read was mine, it didn't matter!

The Unforgettable Response

"The Parasite of Our Class" was the title of my first article published on our school's wall magazine. I had written it in response to the way some of our teachers would make off-color jokes and comments of a sexual nature during lesson time. I didn't think it was appropriate for teachers to treat their students in such a way and so I used the article to get my point across.

At the end of his lesson that afternoon, our geography teacher suddenly pointed at me and said, "So, you think that I am the parasite of our class, yeah?" *Oh, wow!* An unforgettable response from one of my target readers!

The editor of the wall magazine was my classmate, and he felt that the way our geography teacher had attacked me, the writer, was unacceptable. That led to a special editorial meeting, and I attended as their special journalist. The Managing Editor, our Bahasa Indonesia teacher, led the discussion. He closed the meeting with, "So true, dirty language used by students, and even more by a teacher, should be stopped. I am delighted by the fact that the main message of this article hit the target, and I hope no one would become the parasite of our classes anymore." He looked at me and smiled, "Keep writing from your heart."

Indeed, every writer needs an encourager.

A Priceless Resource

My parents always shared their life struggles with us, their children, and together we would bring them to the Lord.

In 1965, my Dad had a small business making tennis and badminton rackets and the factory was at the back of our house. The market was seasonal. One day during the low season, my Mom told us, "We don't have any money left, so let us pray and ask the Lord."

> He looked at me and smiled, "Keep writing from your heart."
>
> Indeed, every writer needs an encourager.

We knelt in a circle and prayed in turn, from the youngest to the oldest. My sister was four years old, I was five, and my brother was nine. When my Dad closed his prayer with an "amen," the doorbell rang. My Dad opened the door, and there stood two Sikh gentlemen. They came in, ordered badminton rackets, and gave him a down payment.

That became a very significant moment in my life. Knowing that God can be trusted and He is the Living God continues to encourage me greatly in times of difficulty. Such *kairos* moments have enriched my life and have become priceless resources for my writing journey.

The Children's Magazine

One afternoon in the year 2000 in Jakarta, someone rang me and said, "Hi, how are you doing? I want to offer you the position of managing editor of the monthly children's magazine, *KiTa* — Christ is the Lord of the Children. Would you please consider it?"

I laughed and replied, "I don't think that you would be able to make me sit and stay on the editor's chair! I am a field person and not someone who could work behind the desk in an office."

He did not give up, and instead offered me the job of co-hosting a children's program broadcasted by a local Christian station where he was director. I decided to accept this offer.

Although I didn't want to take the offer to be the managing editor of the children's magazine, in my daily prayers I could not ignore the still small voice whispering deep down in my heart about that position. One day, he rang me to ask again, "Would you please be the managing editor of *KiTa* magazine?"

"Okay, I will."

"Oh, thank you. This must be God's timing. Our current managing editor just resigned and she said she will be leaving tomorrow."

As a managing editor I had to recruit new writers and create a new devotional book as an insert in the magazine. I also had to write the dialogue for the back-cover comic strip which had become the signature of the magazine.

I was amazed by the fact that when God is the One who puts me in a position, the impossible would be made possible. What had previously seemed impossible from my own limited understanding and point of view had become possible. I even forgot to leave my chair and was almost always working overtime!

Necessary Training

Although I had been doing writing, translating, and editing for the children's magazine, I had never received any training for those tasks. One day, I went to Bandung and met Mary Jane, a missionary who was working as a communicator and lecturer in a theological seminary. She was about to leave Indonesia and to return to her home country because of health issues.

"Please contact H.A. Oppusunggu, the director of Bina Kasih Press in Jakarta. They will be running a training workshop for writers."

> I have come to learn that there is no instant writer. Every writer needs to be an excellent re-writer. This invaluable process has molded us to be humble Christian writers.

It must have been God's prompting. When I rang them, they said they had sent the invitation letter to our previous office address. That was how I was able to attend the "Writing Children's Stories" Workshop by Larry Brook, the writer trainer from Media Associates International (MAI), on March 17 – 23, 2002.

I had never imagined that one day I would meet H.A. Oppusunggu in person. His name has been familiar to me since I was a little girl. He greeted us with his famous negative comments about the writing that we had submitted prior to the training. But Larry did the reverse. He always encouraged us with positive comments first and then followed with suggestions for rewriting.

Smackdown was the title of what I had written. During that workshop, for the first time, I realized that my piece was an article and not a story. I had to switch my mindset from "don't tell" to "describe it." After some rewriting, my article finally became a story!

Larry asked us to read our final stories in turn. When I finished reading my story, Larry said, "Look, Eva really enjoyed her story, and that is important for a writer."

The Writers' Club

Every weekend in August to September 2003, Professor Dr. Miriam Adeney from MAI conducted a serial seminar and workshop on "Writing Articles for Publishing" at the Bina Kasih Press office in Jakarta.

At the end of the seminar and workshop, H.A. Oppusunggu invited Miriam, myself, and some of the Bina Kasih staff to a brief meeting where he said, "As Miriam has suggested, I think we have to have a writers' club as a follow-up to this seminar." Smiling, he looked at me and said, "And I would like to ask this person to be the coordinator of the writers' club that we will facilitate."

I knew that his intention was for me to learn as much as possible, so I accepted his offer. Initially we met once a month. Later on, the meetings became once every fortnight.

H.A. Oppusunggu and Leatha Humes (senior editors of Bina Kasih Press) attended our meetings. They taught us about the elements in a story, and everyone brought a story she or he had written. We then critiqued each other's writing and did our re-writing. There was also one occasion when we had a writers' retreat.

As Miriam had said, "Every writer needs an encourager." So, through the writers' club, we encouraged one another. And I have come to learn that there is no instant writer. Every writer needs to be an excellent re-writer. This invaluable process has molded us to be humble Christian writers.

The Parent-Children Devotional Book

"Now as parents we have come to realize that building up our children's faith is our main responsibility. Is there any book which can help us?" That was the precious result of a questionnaire I had prepared for a parents-and-Sunday-school-teachers' meeting at a church in Jakarta where I had started to work.

"No, unfortunately we don't have any book for it, so we have to make it." In responding to that question, I recruited some writers. Together with Sarwono, the owner of a big printing press who had wholeheartedly supported me in this work, we set up a publishing house, Salt and Light of the World, on August 26, 2003, in a small room I had rented in Jakarta.

We published *peraHU seri 1 — ASALKAN BAPA BERSAMAKU (As Long As the Father Is with Me)*, and *peraHU seri 2 — JANGAN TUNDA, SEGERA TAAT (Don't Delay, Do Obey)*.

Later on, the chair of the Sunday school of another church rang me to ask, "Do you have any children and/or family camp follow-up book?"

"No, unfortunately we don't have that kind of book."

"So, what should we do?"

"We will have to create it."

In responding to that need we published *PELENGKAP peraHU seri 1 — IMAN* (the supplement to peraHU series 1 — FAITH).

In the process of creating, preparing, writing, and publishing these books, the LORD opened my eyes to see that most churches have been focusing on programs and delivering instant messages in their sermons and teachings; even in their Bible studies. Church members do not know how to find the treasure in God's Word anymore, because churches are just too busy with activities and not empowering the people. The LORD helped me to see how dangerous it would be!

In one of the 2004 issues of *BASIS* (a Roman Catholic monthly cultural magazine in Indonesia), they shared their research findings on the devotional life of Christian families in Indonesia. It was so sad to find out that we are lagging far behind when compared to Muslims families. Indonesia is a secular country with the largest Muslim population in the world.

These facts concerned me deeply. They underlined the importance and even the urgency of continuing to publish the devotional book series for parents and children, together with its curriculum for teachers. By using these series, they will know how to find the treasures of God's Word themselves, with the help of the Holy Spirit. They will experience the tremendous joy of finding God's precious truths day by day.

LittWorld 2004

One morning, when I entered H.A. Oppusunggu's office, he asked, "Is there anyone from Bina Kasih Press who would attend LittWorld 2004 in Tagaytay, Manila?"

He looked at me and smiled, "I want you to attend LittWorld 2004. But you have to provide your own funding. Do you have any money for that?"

"No, I don't have any, but it is still several months away, and the Lord can provide it if this is in His plans for me. If not, that's okay, maybe next time."

"I think you would be the first among others here who will get the funding."

He wrote a letter to John Maust, the President of MAI, asking for a scholarship for me to attend LittWorld 2004. I thank God that MAI graciously gave me the opportunity to contribute only USD100 and allowed me to pay on arrival. Prior to the closing of the early bird offer, the Lord amazingly provided all the funds I needed to attend LittWorld 2004. That was my first international conference. I went together with one of the Bina Kasih staff and one of the writers I had recruited when I was working at the children's magazine.

I was amazed by the very humble atmosphere that pervaded LittWorld 2004. Every participant was ready to learn and to share. Ian Darke, one of the speakers, patiently listened to what I was trying to share in my very poor spoken English. I received a very helpful and encouraging one-on-one consultation with Tony Wales from the UK and Mark Carpenter from Brazil. I asked Randy Capp, the trainer for graphic designers, to examine the two devotional books we had published. "All is perfect," he said. And when I asked Rodney Shepherd from Lion Hudson Publishing House, UK, who taught us about "From concept to cover," to have a look, he opened the book and said, "I love this, may we get the copyright? Please send me a rough outline of what this is about."

Yet, back in Jakarta, we had to face the fact that family devotions have become very rare in our Christian families. As Tony Wales, one of the founding members of Lion Hudson Publishing House, said, "You have to go through a very long and very hard journey: you have to educate the church leaders first, and the church leaders have to educate their congregations. But, don't be discouraged, Eva."

In 2005, because we couldn't cover the operational costs anymore, I had to come to the very hard decision of closing the publishing house.

Australia

I had never thought that someday I would be an Australian Permanent Resident and would live in Sydney. I wasn't even interested in moving to Australia. What for?

Yet, I had to follow my Master's plan for my life. In August 2006, I received my Australian Permanent Resident visa and I joined my family in Australia on the 2nd of December.

"Be still, and know that I am God." I read it and was asking my LORD to help me to understand what He meant. I went through a very hard time and experienced culture shock during my three and a half years in Sydney. Through listening and reading *Strength for the Journey*, Joseph Stowell's daily devotional, and reading his book *Radical Reliance*, I began to understand why the LORD had so graciously brought me to Australia. I wrote it as the main message in my entry for MAI's Littworld 2012 writing competition.

May I Come In, Please?[2]

Hi, My Dear Friends in Indonesia,

I am writing this letter to you because it seems you are very busy in the kitchen, and no one hears my "knock, knock" at your door.

I just want to let you know that I am very keen to come in and eat with you. I know that you love me so much, and are preparing the best Indonesian food for me. It's true that I love Indonesian food very much, it's spicy and very delicious. I think you have been worried too much about the food. The most important thing to me is having an intimate relationship with you. I would love a face-to-face table talk with you every morning.

---

[2] This article was awarded a runner-up honorable mention prize in MAI's LittWorld 2012 writing competition. Judges commented, "The message is very basic, very simple, but presented powerfully in the Indonesian context."

And "I love the way the concept of food is used throughout... It is such a creative way to make it fit the Indonesian context and also alludes to the biblical references in the life of Jesus and His teachings."

So, may I come in, please... Just open the door for me, let me come in and stay with you. Let me serve you, I am the host and you are my guest. Just enjoy a lovely time with me, and get to know me better and closer. The more you know me, the more insight you get. It will open your mind and open your eyes.

I know you have learnt by heart that "People do not live by rice alone, but by every word that comes from the mouth of God." Yes, you will enjoy finding the truth. It is sweeter than the best honey in Indonesia. You will love my food the most. You will drink the living water I give you, and you will never thirst.

I am very keen to be your intimate Friend. So that, in the last day I can declare that "I know you."

Much love,
Jesus

One day in December 2009, I had opened the door for Jesus to come in and stay with me. Since that day, I have needed to continually repent in terms of checking my daily Christian walk and refocusing my daily life onto Jesus. Intimacy with Christ become my daily priority.

How could I write according to His heart if I did not start from a heart that was in tune with His?

A Lifetime Impact from Writer to Writer

"No, no, don't make it chronological. Chronology is boring. Write short stories, and then sew it; sew it from story to story." I have kept this precious wise advice of a humble international award-winning writer and trainer from Ghana in my heart since Littworld 2004 in Tagaytay, Philippines.

I ticked a one-on-one consultation with Lawrence Darmani as my first priority option in Littworld 2012, at Brackenhurst, Kenya.

It was 30 minutes per participant. I advised Yahya, another Indonesian writer and editor who had attended Littworld 2012 with me, to take a one-on-one consultation with Lawrence as well, immediately after my session. Lawrence very kindly accepted my request to make it a one-hour session for Yahya and me together.

In answering my question, "How not to be trapped in using the same style in writing based-on-true-story books that we are going to publish?" Lawrence clearly and generously shared his precious writing treasures with us. From his explanations, I came to understand better how to make the pattern and sew it from story to story as he had advised me in 2004. I wrote them all in my notebook and captured what he said in my heart.

I also bought Jerry B. Jenkins' *Writing for the Soul* from the MAI book counter and read it after returning to Jakarta. In addition, I emailed John Maust, and he gave me his invaluable advice when he found out that I was going to write biographies.

The First Biography I Wrote
The warm and sweet voice of my pastor and close friend when I was studying in Yogyakarta, Central Java, Indonesia, was at the other end of the phone call from Jakarta. "Hello Eva, how are you? I need your help. Could you please fly to Perth for one or two weeks? I would like you to write my biography and publish it for me in time for my emeritus service next July."

"Yes, sure, it would be a privilege for me to write the biography for you. And if you agree, I won't make it chronological. What if we write it as short stories and for general readers? Is that all right with you? I'm about to go to Sydney for Christmas, so I can do the interview in Perth in January 2013." He agreed.

I applied all I had learnt from Lawrence, Jerry, and John. I did the interview, transcribed the recordings, wrote and edited the biography, and did the prepress. But we could not meet the July deadline to publish the book for his emeritus service. In the process, I learnt that a book like this has to be published in God's right time. It took ten months to complete the biography, and we launched it in October, 2013, in Jakarta. If we had published the biography by July, we would have regretted it deeply. Thank you so much, LORD!

Do I Have to Lay Down My Passion?

In March 2010 I moved back and stayed in Jakarta for one and a half years. During Christmas 2010, Sarwono and I made the decision to re-commence the "Salt and Light of the World" publishing house in January 2011. We intended to focus on original material from Indonesia, written by local writers. I chose to have a home-based office so that we could minimize the operational costs. That also meant that I could do my work from both Australia and Indonesia.

All went well until my father's fall in November 2013. That made it necessary for me to set aside my job and move back to Sydney to support my parents. I thought it would be temporary, until we had all settled in the new place. After waiting for several weeks and then several months to start writing and publishing again, I found that I had neither the time nor the energy. Yet I trusted that this would be the time for the Author of my life to write His story in me.

> I learnt that a book like this has to be published in God's right time. It took ten months to complete the biography

I was so confused by the conflicting desires within me. Should I stop caring for my parents? Or should I lay down my passion? And for how long? I simply could not imagine a life without the freedom to write. I remember so clearly how the last chapter of *LOVE the LIFE you LIVE* by Les Parrott and Neil Clark Warren had confirmed my calling to be an author when I read the book in 2008. And Mark 10:29-30 was another reminder to be single-minded in giving up everything for Christ's sake and for the Good News. But my parents' needs were very real and immediate.

I found myself incapacitated by depression and spending much of my time in tears. The more I thought about my writing deadlines, the more I spiraled downward.

What Are You Looking Forward To?

One of my friends suggested that I see my doctor to ask for a referral to see a clinical psychologist for help. We started the first session in January 2015. I thank God for guiding me to a very good psychologist who is a believer too.

By the end of my second visit, she asked, "And before you go, my next question is: what are you looking forward to for these coming two to three weeks?"

"I want to write a devotional for MAI's Littworld 2015 writing competition."

"Oh, good, how long will you need in order to finish it?"

"Usually I will write it and have a look the next day to edit it."

"Oh, good, good. Now, what are you looking forward to for the rest of today?"

I had been thinking for a while, "Hmmm, I am looking forward to finalizing the editing of the minutes for the church's general meeting this Saturday."

"Is that something that you have to do, or something that you are looking forward to?"

"Yes, I have to..." I looked at her.

"So, what are you looking forward to? Just simple things that you are looking forward to each day. It's like…oh, I'm looking forward to lying on my bed and reading a book, or maybe enjoying a cup of nice coffee or tea."

"I am looking forward to reading a book in my favorite spot at Parramatta Park."

"Okay, good. So, every day, I want you to ask yourself what is one thing you are looking forward to. Okay?"

I found out that Koorong Books in West Ryde is just 15 minutes away by train from Burwood station. So I decided to go to Koorong Books that afternoon. I was so looking forward to enjoying a book at my favorite spot in Parramatta Park the next morning.

I did it! The next morning, I walked for 15 minutes to the bus stop across the golf course from my place, and I took the free shuttle bus. When I arrived at my destination, I alighted from the bus and walked across the Eels Rugby Club car park, stepping over its very low fence to get into Parramatta Park.

I was so happy to see my favorite spot again; a place of solitude near the Parramatta River bank. There was a fresh breeze blowing, the birds were singing beautifully, and I could smell the newly mown green grass as I sat on the bench enjoying the shade of the Jacaranda trees. I felt so good!

This worked really well. Every day I looked forward to going to Parramatta Park and having my brunch or lunch there. Some days I would read a book and other days I would journal on my tablet. It gave me a kind of hope day by day, and I caught a glimpse of how to love myself the way Jesus taught us in the Gospels. As I found my deep needs met, I also began to regain the energy to do other things better.

I visited the Littworld Online website and I found that I was too late for the 2015 writing competition. I had also been thinking of writing up the chapter about my writing journey, but I wasn't sure if even that opportunity would still be open.

Grace Works

On Thursday, February 5, 2015, at 12:40am, I saw a new email in my inbox, I opened it on my smartphone. The subject was "Asian Authors Journey Book."

Dear Eva,
How are you? And your father?

I know you dread receiving emails from me because I will be chasing you for your article. But I do need to find out from you one way or the other whether you will be contributing a chapter to our book. I need to start prepress work because I would like to have the book published by June.

I look forward to hearing from you!

Bernice
Chair, MAI-Asia

I opened my laptop and typed out a reply.

Dear Bernice,
Thank you so much for asking and being so gracious to me. I thought I have lost the opportunity to contribute a chapter for this book, since I know previously that it will get published on March.

I have been depressed and have seen a clinical psychologist to get help — "mental health plan" — in the hope that I can still pursue my passion in my current situation. ... I have seen my psychologist twice, and finalizing my one chapter for this book is what I am looking forward to having in these two weeks, as a part of the therapy as well.

Your email has sparked the hope in my heart. Thank you. And sure I will take this opportunity with a grateful heart. I will try to finalize writing this one chapter as soon as possible, and am wondering if two weeks from now would be okay for you.

The Lord is so gracious. Thanks again, Bernice. I am looking forward to hearing from you.

With a grateful heart,
Eva

Thirteen minutes later, I received her response.

Dear Eva,
I am so glad I was prompted to write to you. May God grant you strength and intervene in your healing. I will continue to pray more specifically for you.

Two weeks is fine. Also glad that this project can give you a short-term goal to work towards.

Wishing you every blessing,
Bernice

So there you are. You would not be reading this chapter if the writer had not experienced grace upon grace extended to her time and again.

Last night I sent an email to Bernice.

Thanks for continuing to pray for me, I have been progressing well in my writing and my recovery. I am still writing. I have already done more than 4000 words, but I don't think I can submit it tonight. I do hope tomorrow I can finish it and will send it to you. Is that okay for you? Thanks again, Bernice.

She replied,

I'm glad to hear that you're writing and that you're almost done! That is great news. Tomorrow is fine!

Grace works indeed!

FINDING MY VOICE

EMILY has written over 30 books, ranging from picture books to social studies readers and illustrated e-titles. She is the first outside North America to win three medals in children's books at the Independent Publisher Book Awards, the world's largest book awards, and 1st in Southeast Asia to win the Moonbeam Children's Book Award (where she received a Gold Medal). She also received the Honorable Mention Award at Writer's Digest Self-Published Book Awards in 2012 and was a Finalist for SCBWI's Crystal Kite Award 2013 (Asia/India/Middle East Region). Her books have been published in Singapore, Malaysia, China, Korea and Indonesia, and also crossed over to animation and theatre.

Emily was named Mediacorp's Singapore Woman Award Honoree 2013 for inspiring readers through her children's books and her memoir *Finding My Voice*. Emily graduated from writing for children to having one of her own. She's now also full-time mum to her energetic preschooler who inspired her blog Mum-Mum's The Word (mummumstheword.wordpress.com) where she blogs on parenting and writing.

My journey of finding my voice as an author in 2007 began with the story of finding my voice.

It started once upon a time, over 15 years ago, at the end of 1998.

Ben and I had recently married and moved into our new home. He was doing well at an American bank and my career was just at the point of taking off. Life was full of promise.

Shortly after, I woke up one day and found that the Grinch had stolen my voice.

Initially, my voice sounded muffled, like the result of a bout of crying. Then it sounded like I was having a sore throat and, soon, it looked like a case of laryngitis. As weeks passed, I sounded increasingly short of breath, like someone having asthma. Over the span of a few months, it deteriorated to a stage where I had trouble pronouncing my words. Air, instead of sound, came out of my mouth. It took a lot of effort to be understood and I sounded like someone at the end of a very bad overseas phone connection. All the time. At my lowest point, people could only make out about three out of 10 words that I was saying.

Because of the strange erratic nature of this voice affliction, I was misunderstood at every turn because I had trouble getting words out. A simple 5-minute call to the Kentucky Fried Chicken hotline translated into a 20-minute exercise. Buying air tickets through the airline call centers was a bane because it was always met with "Ma'am, what country are you from? We cannot understand. Can you speak English?" When I told a taxi driver to take me to Holland Village (next to where I lived), it sounded like "H...er Ph...igh" and so the taxi driver almost drove me to Hotel Phoenix.

I was later diagnosed with Abductor Spasmodic Dysphonia. Spasmodic Dysphonia, a distant cousin of Parkinson's Disease, is termed as such because the voice waxes and wanes from moment to moment in a spasmodic fashion. It appeared that I might have been one-of-a-kind in Singapore with the rare form of this rare disorder. I usually like to be first in line but I wasn't thrilled to be a forerunner in this department.

Like Dorothy and her friends, the Cowardly Lion, the Scarecrow and the Tin Man, in L. Frank Baum's *The Wizard of Oz*, my journey similarly took me in search of voice, courage, clarity of thought and a new heart. It led me on a deeper search for meaning in life and discovery of a new and different kind of voice. A voice that emerged from the written word.

My journey down the yellow brick road in search of a cure took me from electromagnetic therapy with a sports medicine doctor to Chinese acupuncture, from weekly speech therapy sessions in a Singapore hospital to my first Botox injection at New York's Mount Sinai Hospital. Botox provided temporary relief by paralyzing my vocal cord muscles every few months. But there was no permanent cure. With answers from man coming up short, I started looking towards Heaven for answers.

At the invitation of friends and colleagues, Ben and I started visiting different churches throughout the island. We frequented one church which conducted weekly services where many were prayed for and were known to have recovered from their illnesses. A seed of faith was sown in my heart from listening to those who had gone forward during the services to share stories of their recovery. I secretly wanted to be among these people. But it wasn't my turn to speak yet. I had to wait patiently for my turn.

> With answers from man coming up short, I started looking towards Heaven for answers.

Small droplets of water can wear down even the hardest rock over time. So, progressively, each small negative experience (from being scolded or mocked by another person who couldn't hear me) added up to a point where my self-confidence was eroded completely. Before long, Fear, Worry and Despair took residence in my life. Self-worth and Independence were crowded out and moved elsewhere. So, at the end of each day, I curled up in bed, tired and desperate, crying out to the One whom I believed could hear me. I pleaded for a voice from above.

I did not hear an audible voice from above. I did not encounter any dramatic "burning bush" experiences like Moses did in the desert. I struggled, like Jacob, the patriarch of Israel, who wrestled with a stranger in the middle of the night till his hip was broken. I wrestled with God over my broken voice. And slowly, the voice in my heart gently prompted me: *Let go. Stop struggling.*

At that time, my job had become the lifebuoy I clung to, for fear of sinking into oblivion if I were to let go. It was the fear of becoming a nobody. A nobody defeated by a strange voice disorder. A nobody who might not get another job, or even an interview, because of a non-functioning voice. But there was also a new restlessness stirring in me. A simple dream to do something new. Something that could fire up my lost passion. It was time to let go. It was time to step out in faith. It was now only a matter of timing.

A few months later, my company had a change of ownership. It offered the closure I needed so I took that opportunity to leave on completion of its sale in late 2005. I had no idea where I was going. I thought I would give myself a year or two to smell the roses. But, at the back of my mind, some nagging doubts, including Ben's concerns, lingered. Without direction, would I swim or sink? Without the social interaction at work which had kept me marginally afloat, would I sink into a depressive state? Or could I trust God to pull me up if I went down? Only time would tell.

The year 2007 was my awakening — for my faith, my voice and my passion for the written word. It was almost ten years after I had been first afflicted with SD.

Someone I met at a church Bible study class recommended that I read Kenneth Hagin Jr's writings. I went to the bookstore and stumbled on Kenneth Hagin Jr's book, *Overflow — Living Above Life's Limits*, which was centered on the promise in John 10:10 where Jesus said, "The thief comes to steal, kill and destroy. I came so that they may have and enjoy life, and have it in abundance (to the full, till it overflows)."

This book, in essence, taught me three things: First, I could go through life focusing on what I do not have (normal voice, career prospects, "what if's?") or I could focus on the blessings that I have and the possibilities that await me. Second, I could hold on to my self-imposed limitations and "half-empty" negative attitude or I could choose to line up my thinking with God's word. John 10:10 said that God wants me to live life to the full. Third, I could stay defeated by my weaknesses, shortcomings and failures or I could take hold of the greatness of God in my thought life and change my attitude.

> I had no idea where I was going. I thought I would give myself a year or two to smell the roses. But, at the back of my mind, some nagging doubts, including Ben's concerns, lingered.

For the first time since SD robbed me of my vision of my future, I saw life with new possibilities. I started to believe that God was for me and not against me. I started to believe that I could live above life's limitations, or more like my self-imposed limitations. I knew that I had to let go of the negative thoughts that had become deeply rooted in me. It was time to stop listening to the voices in my head that told me I couldn't have, shouldn't have and couldn't be. It was time for me to have a new voice.

In early 2007, I read in the newspapers about a publishing initiative for children's books organized by the Singapore Book Council.

It was different from the usual writing competitions where winners received a cash prize and a certificate. It was more. Award recipients were given a grant to publish their winning manuscripts. Entries had to include a manuscript, marketing and promotion plan, a business plan, and budget on how we would publish and market our books. This felt like a full-time job, but with a project budget which was a few zeros less than what I used to work on. In my previous job, I worked on hotel projects and acquisitions with a leading luxury hotel company. This time, I would be building a book, my book. Could this open the way into a new industry and a new vocation? It was a fleeting thought but I decided to throw my heart and energy into the competition.

I knew nothing and no one in the publishing industry. So, I started out by spending many hours in the bookstores and libraries, seeking inspiration on what to write. In the end, I decided on a children's picture book because it required the fewest words. After weeks of reflection and research, my first manuscript, *Prince Bear & Pauper Bear*, was birthed. There would be one perfect-looking teddy bear. The other bear would be the sad one with mismatched eyes and a poorly stitched coat. And he had to have no mouth, for some reason. Children's books have to rhyme, I told myself. So I forced the story into 32 stanzas.

I brought my manuscript to my two little nieces. As it turned out, I was no Dr Seuss and the result was discouraging. Six-year-old Annabel yawned, several times.

"Do you like the story?" I asked.

Annabel squirmed and would not look me in the eye. Four-year-old Isabelle tried to rip up my manuscript.

I went home deflated. My first taste of rejection was bitter. And it was from my six-year-old niece who adored me. I went to the library and borrowed titles along the lines of *How to Write Children's*

Picture Books. Several drafts later, I read the manuscript to Annabel again, with trepidation.

"*Kooma*, I like the story. Can you read it again?"

I was elated. My manuscript had found acceptance with its first reader!

"*Kooma*, does that mean that he cannot speak?"

In my story, the toymaker forgot to stitch Pauper Bear a mouth. I had not actually followed through how that affected the sad little bear. Following my six-year-old niece's comment, it became the most important symbol in my story.

> I went home deflated. My first taste of rejection was bitter. And it was from my six-year-old niece who adored me.

Prince Bear & Pauper Bear became a winner in the Book Council competition and my first published book. The next five months marked the awakening of a passionate voice. I woke up each morning filled with anticipation as I worked to complete writing and publishing my book as part of this Initiative. There were some negative voices along the way. Ben, my very resolute husband, reminded me to ignore all the people who told me I couldn't and I shouldn't. And he told me to stay true to my own voice.

I published my first book under my Mustard Seed Books imprint, inspired by the Parable of the Mustard Seed in Matthew 13:32 of the Bible where Jesus said, "Though it (the mustard seed) is the smallest of all your seeds, yet when it grows, it is the largest of garden plants and becomes a tree, so that the birds of the air come and perch on its branches."

Prince Bear & Pauper Bear became the first in Southeast Asia to win an award at the IPPY awards in its 12 years of existence. A group of judges at the world's largest book awards had brought sunshine to my little "mustard seed" book.

Like the proverbial mustard seed in the parable, I started to experience my first growth. The launch of *Prince Bear & Pauper Bear* brought me to a crossroad where I had to confront SD head on. Up until the final stages of publishing the book, I had not realized that I had subconsciously written my own story. Now I had to decide if I wanted to talk about it.

"What was the inspiration for the story?" the first reporter asked.

Oh no! Why did I have to write my personal story? I chided myself. *Now I have to talk about it!*

Maybe there's a reason why you wrote the story, came the second thought. *Maybe you were meant to talk about it.*

After debating both thoughts in my head, I decided to listen to the gentler voice.

"I started out like Prince Bear, expecting life to be perfect," I said. "But I ended up feeling like Pauper Bear after I came down with SD, without a mouth and voice to speak of. But along the way, Pauper Bear experiences kindness from various people, and is basically given a second chance..."

After the flurry of activity launching *Prince Bear & Pauper Bear*, I found myself facing a blank page. *What now?* I asked myself.

After experiencing a high in the previous six months, I didn't expect to fall to a low so quickly. I tried writing a second manuscript, but I couldn't birth it. *The Tale of Rusty Horse* was about an old forgotten rocking horse that longs to be real so that children will ride on it again. He eventually comes to a point where he has to choose between his desire to be a crowd favorite or being true to himself. It was at that point that I grappled with validation from the first readers of the manuscript.

"I don't like the fairy," said one friend. "He appears too conveniently to grant wishes."

"The sacrificial love ending may be difficult for children to understand," said another friend.

"Too didactic," said my then literary agent.

My first book was a success. It was now looking like my last. I was thrilled to have my first book. Now, new expectations overshadowed my second.

My self-determined two-year sabbatical was also coming to an end and I had no idea what I wanted to do next.

Should I just ask my ex-bosses for my job back? Stick with the familiar and return to the hotel industry? Or should I continue to write — take a step of faith down the path less travelled?

Little did I realize that I had turned into Rusty Horse, grappling with the need for public validation. As I stood at the crossroads of indecision, my second manuscript also struggled to see light of day.

Then, three voices encouraged me.

"I like the story," said Ben. "Just go ahead and publish the book."

"The manuscript is okay," said my friend Gail. "You just need to smoothen out the rough bits."

And the youngest voice blew me away after I read her the manuscript and asked her to tell me what this story was about.

"It's about an old rocking horse that learns to be at peace with himself," said Christina, my seven-year-old goddaughter, nonchalantly in between mouthfuls of *ice kachang*. Her spot-on comments stopped me running around in circles of indecision. I made peace with Rusty, the dark horse, and published his story.

The Tale of Rusty Horse galloped off with a Gold medal at the Moonbeam Children's Book Awards, the first in Southeast Asia to ever win a Moonbeam medal in one of the fastest-growing US-based Children's Book Awards. The "dark horse" book which almost bowed to crowd opinion and didn't see the light of day was singled out for special mention in the competition's results announcement. It was a symbolic win for me. It was like Heaven's nod to my new station in life, telling me to let go of my past. I finally made peace with my decision to pursue the uncharted path of an author in Singapore.

After the publishing of my first two books, I followed up with two more books. I had not intended to write my personal stories. Yet subconsciously, I had done so in all four of my books. Faith and passion had been the driving voice.

Prince Bear & Pauper Bear had been my "coming out" story. Pauper Bear, my main character, did not have a mouth and could not speak for himself. Yet, he gave voice to my reservoir of emotions, built up from years of silence about my voice struggles. This teddy bear tale summed up in 800 simple words what I had trouble articulating for a decade.

The Tale of Rusty Horse, my "struggle" book, was written at a time when I struggled with letting go of all that had happened following SD. And so, Rusty the rocking horse became very fixated with crowd opinion. He wanted everyone to like and accept him. But

Rusty finally realized that he had the power to choose. He chose to stay true to himself. In doing so, he realized that there was a purpose for his station in life and he finally experienced peace. Like Rusty, I discovered the power of choice and found peace in my decision to take the write trail instead of the familiar corporate work route.

Just Teddy was my "realization" story, inspired by acceptance of myself. Teddy went to great lengths to blend in with the polar bears, pandas, and finally the penguins. In the process, he made a big mess of himself; he almost lost his true identity. And so it was for me too. Like Teddy, I struggled hard to find acceptance after I came down with SD. Once I opened my mouth, I sounded different and people looked at me differently. It made me feel like I didn't belong with the crowd. And so, I tried so hard to sound normal. It was only through faith that I discovered that, despite my flaws and defects, I am loved by my Creator just as I am and, in the words of Psalm 139, I am "fearfully and wonderfully made."

> Circumstances in life may have shaped me and left their mark on me. But I am made of the stuff that fills me on the inside.

My fourth book, *Bunny Finds the Right Stuff*, was inspired by the recognition that we are shaped by the things we fill our lives with and what we believe in. It was my "revelation" and "interconnectedness" story. Bunny believed that he had missed out on more stuffing. He thought he was loved less than the other toys and had therefore been given less. So, he set out to right the wrong; to make himself better. As he ran around stuffing himself with inappropriate fillings, each experience and wrong path he took left a mark on him. Bunny was surrounded by friends who gave him room to grow but also stepped in when necessary. Through this, he finally found the stuff he had been looking for — the stuff of love and friendship. He also learnt that his floppiness was not from lack but from years of being loved and hugged to bits by the toymaker. Like Bunny, I stopped searching for reasons why I had woken up one day without much voice to speak of. I came to realise that a weak nervous voice did not make me a weak nervous person. Circumstances in life may have shaped me and left their mark on me. But I am made of the stuff that fills me on the inside.

Feedback from friends and readers fuelled my newfound passion in writing. On the day after the launch party of my first book, *Prince Bear & Pauper Bear*, my friend Joanne called me up to tell me her three-year-old daughter's response when she read her the story at bedtime.

"Every night when I put Vicky to bed, she would say, 'Goodnight Mummy'," Joanne said. "Last night, she said, 'Goodnight Pauper Bear, don't be sad, I will be your friend'."

At my first public book reading, I asked the audience, "What did Pauper Bear discover at the end of the story?"

"The boy had enough room in his heart for two teddy bears," replied an adult voice. "It's like how Daddy loves both of you just as much," said the father to two young children seated on his lap.

With each book launched, friends, acquaintances and strangers would email or text me with how they felt about the books and encourage me to continue writing. Two people in particular, who left a deep impression, were readers I had never even met or spoken to.

The first was a lady in her 20s who shared in an email about how *Just Teddy* had touched her. She connected with the main character — looking to fit in and getting all messed up along the way. She had struggled with issues of insecurity, looks, and identity throughout her life. As she read how *Just Teddy* was cleaned up and discovered his identity as a one-of-a-kind bear, her heart leapt as it made her realise that she too was unique, "fearfully and wonderfully made."

The second person was a veteran banker who had stopped work two years earlier to support his then five-year-old son, diagnosed with possible Asperger's Syndrome, through therapy during his most formative years. He wrote a long poignant email which included the following extracts:

> I had survived hours of contract negotiations in my previous job, but I was now afraid to read a picture book to an audience consisting mainly of children.

"My wife bought me your book and shared in a letter that she felt similarities between me and my son and Rusty Horse and the handicapped boy. Although I had a chance to return back to my corporate life (earlier this year) to become a 'real horse' again, I also had the option of remaining as Rusty the rocking horse to continue to provide my son the love and support that he needs. In a sense, your book helped me realize my continued role to my son and allowed me to be confident in my decision not to return to full time work till 2012 when he goes to Primary One.

Although many have said that giving up my career is a sacrifice, I feel that going back to work is also a sacrifice in terms of my son's development as he has his whole life ahead of him. To me, there is only that much more I can do at work but there is much more that I can do for him.

It is not easy as it's a lonely and sometimes humbling path as socially, it is not very accepted in our culture for a man to take on this role. But on hindsight, I am glad to have taken this road less travelled as it makes all the difference.... I enjoy my moments with him and he has helped me grow as much as I may have helped him...I wanted to write this email to let you know the inspiration and hope and wonderful message your books can bring."

That these little picture books could have connected with adults in such a real way amazed me beyond my understanding. It revealed to me the power of the written word. It encouraged me that I was on the right track in taking the "write" trail in this chapter of my life.

When I first wrote *Prince Bear & Pauper Bear*, I had decided that I would not be involved in any promotional work for my book. I was afraid of public speaking and even more so after my voice affliction. I wanted to be one of those authors holed up somewhere tapping away on the keyboard in the most suitable attire for this vocation — pajamas. The last thing I wanted was interaction with readers who would invariably ask questions about my strange voice.

Then shortly after my first book was published, my friend Joanne asked if I would like to do a charity reading at her client's revamped food outlet located at a high-traffic area of a shopping center.

"Can your client provide a microphone? I don't think I can read above the noise level in a shopping center."

"I'm not sure they have one," Joanne said. "But don't worry. If we have to, we'll buy one!"

I also found that I had trouble sustaining a storytelling voice throughout the 800 words of my book. I had survived hours of contract negotiations in my previous job, but I was now afraid to read a picture book to an audience consisting mainly of children.

I called my friend Gail next. "Can I borrow your children to read with me? I don't think I can read alone."

She readily agreed and worked out reading parts between her children and me.

I sent emails to family members and friends and rounded up close to 20 supporters. "Just clap regardless of how I read, okay?" I told everyone.

When the event started, Ben acted as my emcee. It also helped that I was reading with a line-up of adorable-looking children. *At least the crowd will clap for them.* The familiar faces around me brought much cheer. Slowly, curious onlookers stopped to watch and a bigger crowd gathered and responded with enthusiasm. I passed my first book-reading event without passing out from anxiety.

Following that first book reading, many more public events followed. The support of family and friends at many of my initial book events and through my writing journey lifted me to a level where I dared to venture out alone for speaking engagements. Slowly, I went from reading to audiences of 20 to speaking to student populations of up to 2,000. And I did so with prayer and confidence that God would give me the voice and fortitude to speak.

> **As I talked less and listened more, I discovered that everyone has problems. Everyone struggles with issues in their lives.**

Through these events, I also came to discover the power of the spoken word. I had conversations with many people who were strangers from the onset; we connected and shared our personal stories without reservation. As I talked less and listened more, I discovered that everyone has problems. Everyone struggles with issues in their lives. Some encountered single clear defining moments which helped them overcome their setbacks. Others, like me, went through a more protracted journey dotted with minor intersections which moved them along. Some came out stronger; others continued to struggle. Although we were different, yet in many ways, we were similar. We shared the same emotions and fears. And through that, we took courage from one other's life journeys. We connected and left our unique thumbprints on each other's lives.

After seven years of Botox injections to my vocal muscles to help me sustain a voice, I chose not to follow up with further treatment after my last injection in late 2006. Someone from a church Bible study class whom I met for the first time had prophesied that I would recover and, for the first time, I believed. Since then, beyond understanding, my voice has strengthened and it is as good as recovered. It is better than it had ever been even with my best days of medical treatment. A doctor friend specializing in rehabilitative medicine described my voice as "functionally normal."

Like Pauper Bear, I too had sat in my dark corner, feeling incomplete and unloved. But Pauper Bear was restored and given a voice. My voice too has been restored. And it came back strengthened in the Word. It is a voice found in God's Word.

As I continue this chapter in my life as an author, I do so with the assurance that God, the Author of Life, has a good storyline for me.

Credits:
Extracted with permission from *Finding My Voice: A True Story of Setbacks, New Beginnings and Toy Characters* by Emily Lim (Singapore: Write Editions, 2011).

JACOB'S LADDER

MO FEI is the pen name of Teresina Chen. She was born in Taiwan, moved to the US when she was 18, and currently lives in Los Angeles with her family. She is a full-time writer and speaker, and also a founder of the Genesis Chinese Writing Ministry Institute which promotes writings on faith. Mo Fei is an award-winning writer who has won several major literary awards in Taiwan, both for short fiction and essays. Her works have appeared in various literary magazines and newspapers in Taiwan, China and North America.

Seeking My Life-Altar

As a Chinese girl who lived in daydreams and only knew to follow the path society had charted for women, my only ambition from a young age was to be married. It was strange, though; while this goal was not very visionary, it was still very difficult to achieve.

Yet, even as I went through some rough patches in life, I found that "where there's a will, there's a way." I married myself off at last at the age of 29.

Back in high school, when we had to choose specializations, I had blindly gone with the flow and studied whatever would be easiest to land a job. So I chose business. After graduation, I came to America when my father's diplomatic work led him here. When faced with the task of selecting a major in college, an aunt suggested that, "Girls should study either nursing or accounting." This decision was very easy for me; I was afraid of blood, so naturally I chose to major in accounting.

Four years later, I graduated and worked as an accounting manager at a bank in Washington, D.C. After a year, however, I found that this existence of chasing deadlines and churning out reports was very tiring. In addition, the interpersonal conflicts and various complexities of office politics were too much for me to deal with, so I considered changing careers. Again, someone offered a plan, saying, "In America, Chinese people study either accounting or computers which does not require a whole lot of English language. If accounting didn't work for you, then you should switch to computer science." I was a person without independent thinking, therefore, computer science it was. After graduation, I landed a job as a systems engineer at Hughes Aircraft Company in Southern California.

At that time, Hughes Aircraft Company had two people to an office. At the end of the workday, I would turn off my desk lamp and exchange a "See you tomorrow!" with my colleague. One day, however, as I was turning that lamp knob and preparing to say goodbye, out of nowhere a thought appeared: would I always be in the same office, at the same desk, turning off the same lamp each day and saying to my colleague, "See you tomorrow!" until I was 65 years old?

At this moment, suddenly clearly seeing the horizon of my entire life, I was shocked. It seemed as if in my whole life, I had never truly pondered and made any decisions about my life. I had only followed the tracks set by society, graduating, finding a job, getting married. Then what about the next step? Would I go on like this until I was 65?

That moment of awakening triggered my midlife crisis. I just did not know: Who was I? What kind of person did I want to become? The first half of my life, I had only followed the paths many people in society had already taken. Now because of this crisis, I started pursuing a "life direction;" pondering what kind of person I really wanted to become.

> In the letter, she said that literature possessed special characteristics that allowed it to permeate culture deeply, broadly, and across time and space.

While searching, I thought: Who inspires admiration in me? I discovered that it was those people who were very clear about what they wanted to do in their lives and would live and die for it. Many years later, they became authorities in their field. They were not like me, who in the past only parroted other people, switching careers here and there, and reaching half my years without identifying my path. And so I began actively seeking my own life-altar.

Even so, on the eve of my wedding, as yet single but about to be wed, I suddenly felt a surge of emotion that I had to express. So I emulated Taiwanese author Xiao-Feng Zhang and wrote the piece "Regarding Stepping onto the Red Carpet" (Chinese culture traditionally uses red as the main theme color for weddings). I submitted it to my fellowship's small publication, *Xing Yuan* (this article was the predecessor of my book *Two Ends of the Red Carpet*). Unexpectedly, this article garnered responses from quite a few singles.

At that time, *Xing Yuan*'s editor-in-chief was a dear sister, Maria Ma, who was only 17 years old but possessing an uncommon life perspective. In a long letter to me, she revealed a concept I had never heard before: "writing ministry." This concept added a layer of serious meaning to an essay, which for me was just a way to express my emotions. In the letter, she said that literature possessed special characteristics that allowed it to permeate culture deeply, broadly, and across time and space. If writing could be considered a form of "ministry," a calling, how far-reaching could the influence be for transforming the heart and spirit and conveying the Gospel? I was moved to start exploring this "writing ministry."

With the hot-bloodedness of youth, I was very moved at the time and fearlessly wrote another article, submitting it to the North American Chinese publication *Ambassadors for Christ Magazine*. The article was rejected. The editor at that time was Pastor Edwin Su, who later founded Chinese Overseas Campus Ministries. He not only rejected the submission, he also very humorously attached an application form for the China Evangelical Seminary extension course for writing soon to be held in Los Angeles, and wrote: "It would be better to get some training." It was the first time in my life that having a submission rejected made me so happy, because there was still hope, and a way out had been shown to me.

So I obediently registered for the writing class. In the class, my literary perspective was broadened in an instant. With Pastor Edwin Su's unique humorous and vivid teaching method, I felt refreshed every time I went to class, and each night I would return home feeling spiritually sated.

In that course, Pastor Edwin Su had a set pattern: at the beginning of every class, he would share a devotional. As a teacher, I have now inherited this tradition; because I know that this short time of sharing may sometimes have more influence over a person's life decisions than the course content. I personally discovered my life-altar from one of these pre-class devotionals.

Once, Pastor Edwin Su shared the way of the writing ministry: "Every Christian has the obligation to share the Gospel, and when you keep fulfilling this obligation, God will grant you the gifts you need in ministry; when you keep exercising these gifts to a certain point, you will need to focus on one area; and when you do this to a certain degree, you can walk onto the path of full-time ministry."

This sharing inspired me in an instant. In the past, I thought that writers needed to rely on talent, which was the gift of only a few brilliant people. I had not thought that if we think of writing as a ministry, we could ask God for the gifts through diligence. In fact, when I thought more deeply about it, the emergence of "gifts" is purely for the needs of ministry. This could overlap but did not necessarily have to equate with innate ability and talent.

> I had not thought that if we think of writing as a ministry, we could ask God for the gifts through diligence.

That night, a fire was ignited in my heart, and after I got home, I excitedly talked about it with my husband the entire night. It felt like I had seen Jacob's ladder to heaven: there were many people going up and down that ladder, and that ladder was my "writing ministry." I talked the whole night and couldn't fall asleep. I guess you can say that that was when I first heard my calling to the "writing ministry."

Earlier that night, when Pastor Su shared the devotional with us, he had said that whoever had a burden for it could talk to him after class. There were more than 40 students in the class, but it seemed as if I was the only one excited to speak with Pastor Su. He suggested that I first enter a seminary and select courses to equip myself. At first, I was just passionate and felt that I could try my hand at this. Unexpectedly, about a year after I entered seminary, I discovered that serving God in this area full-time was precisely the life-altar I aspired to. I then quit my job and started to study and serve in this area full-time.

Confirming My Calling

However, it was not all smooth sailing after I had been called to the writing ministry. At that time, my church was setting up branch churches, and we had a total of five Mandarin service pastors; every one of them had discussions with me about going to seminary for ministry. But each pastor had his own understanding of the writing ministry, and I was quite confused. Some believed that the writing ministry required studying theology, and not just studying theology but also getting a doctoral degree and becoming a theologian. Others said that knowing Chinese was enough for the writing ministry; studying theology was optional, and taking care of church newsletters was good enough. All this splashed a basin of cold water on my new passion.

I didn't know at the time, but my church was not the only one that did not completely understand the writing ministry. Actually, the entire Chinese church circle did not have a very clear idea about the role and nature of a writing ministry in God's kingdom. I had originally thought if I were willing to serve the Lord, I would receive support and encouragement from the pastors, but these different opinions actually blurred that image of the heavenly ladder that had been so clear to me.

Furthermore, because I intended to quit my job and go to seminary, my parents were naturally strongly opposed to it. My parents were not Christians and absolutely could not comprehend the meaning of ministry. They only knew that I was giving up what the world considered a safe and stable avenue, and was choosing to walk on an unpopular narrow path. My mother and I had been very close. Living on two different continents for the past ten years, I would send her weekly letters and I treated them almost as diary entries; there was nothing I couldn't discuss with her. My mother was my confidante and my best friend. But now, because I wanted to quit my job, go to seminary, and devote myself to full-time writing work, my mother hung up the phone on me and refused to reply to my letters. She even said to me, "If I had known that you would do this today, why would I have supported you until you got a master's degree?" Her opposition was so fierce that she even wanted to end our mother-daughter relationship. Now that I am a mother, I can understand better how worried and hurt a mother feels when her child chooses a different life path. But at that time, it was agony.

> Now, because I wanted to quit my job, go to seminary, and devote myself to full-time writing work, my mother hung up the phone on me and refused to reply to my letters.

In the meantime, my father was afraid of my being misled and becoming obsessed, so he expressly flew over to America from Taiwan. My sorrowful parents suspected that perhaps my husband, who had been a Christian for many years, had "done something" and clouded my thinking, resulting in this situation. But after my father came to America and discovered that this was not the case, he took my husband aside and said, "Mo Fei is too willful; don't just go along with whatever she wants to do."

But my ever-mild and easygoing husband had his own set of ideas. He replied to my father, "When I was growing up, I never saw a birthday cake on the table; my family was so poor I had lost the privilege to dream, so now I don't even have the ability to dream. But you provided an environment for Mo Fei that gave her the privilege to dream; I am willing to support her in achieving her dream in God's Kingdom." At that time, I knew nothing of this dialogue between them.

I had thought that after receiving my calling, I would live gloriously and radiantly, but here I encountered many internal troubles and outside aggressions; there was a huge gap between reality and my expectations. Just like a boat that has been rocked, I desperately needed support from people around me. So I hoped that my husband could, as he usually did, provide some extraordinary spiritual insight to support and encourage me. But after he had given this amazing speech to my father behind my back, he calmly and reasonably said to me, "I'm sorry, but unless you first clarify your calling, I am unable to support you."

These words that lacked warmth and humanity, in addition to the obstacles all around me, knocked my confidence and faith back to zero. I had thought that many people would applaud and send me onto this path of ministry, but now I faced so many questions and roadblocks. "How could this happen? Why are things like this?" I often asked God in my devotions during that time. Then one day, God replied:

> "Who shall separate us from the love of Christ? Shall trouble or hardship or persecution or famine or nakedness or danger or sword?" (Romans 8:35)

This Bible verse woke me up at once. Who shall separate me from the love of Christ? If my calling were truly from God, why did I need confirmation from people? Was I sure the calling came from God? Or did I simply want to fulfill the literary dreams of my youth? In the final analysis, did I want to write for the Lord, or for my own literary dream?

I then spent several days praying and asking God to continue to give me words of confirmation. During this process, my belief seemed to be rebuilt little by little from the ABCs of our faith. And my calling matured from the initial rush of passion into a decision for lifelong commitment. At the time, I did not know all this was part of God's greater intent.

In the area of a writing ministry, I did not have many footsteps to follow, especially for the Chinese language; nor was it something affirmed by many Chinese churches. It was even less likely for readers to come up and say that reading my words somehow strengthened their faith. Everything was done under a solitary lamp, before God, with each word faithfully written down. Just think: I was unable to see even a face, yet by faith believed that my own writing would help some souls and nurture someone's heart. How much perseverance did this require? It is only because I was certain I had been called to this ministry that I could hold fast in later days when I encountered many setbacks.

> This is the nature of callings — doing what God has called you to do and not questioning whether you are enough, whether you can do it, and whether there is fruit. This is faithfulness.

Especially when I first started to explore writing, I had many struggles. I didn't have enough Chinese vocabulary to use, as I had lived in America for many years, and I had to look up the Chinese vocabulary I needed from an English dictionary. I could not master my pen yet, and for a long time, I submitted articles only to have them rejected; I suffered many refusals and rejections.

Actually, the writing ministry is like preaching; both require practice. The difference is that newly graduated ministers may be unfamiliar with preaching, but churches will always provide a pulpit for practice opportunities. But the difficulty with writing is that there is no *de facto* platform for publication. A rejection is a rejection, and when the writing is not published, it can't even touch one soul, so the ministry result is zero. During that period, there was no one to give me pointers, so I had to figure it out by myself. This is why I later had the burden to teach writing and help some people walk into fewer dead ends.

However, in that dark age of article rejections, it just so happened that many people knew I had quit my high-paying job at Hughes Aircraft Company to devote myself to writing. So they would ask, "Where are the articles? Where were they published?" Even when they were published, the immature literature would raise questions: "You call this kind of article ministry?" Basically, I could not produce a ministry record that bore fruits, and it seemed I could not give an account of myself.

In addition, many people did not have a clear idea of what a writing ministry was. In the beginning, my church gave me a scholarship to support my studies in seminary. But a year later, the church set new scholarship policies and said that, after me, they would no longer support any seminary students besides those focusing on pastoral ministry. I could see that the identity of literature ministers was still undefined and had no set position.

At that time, Pastor Silas Chan, a professor at Logos Evangelical Seminary and veteran in the writing ministry of publishing exegetical books, heard about my situation and asked to speak with me. He spent a whole evening asking me where exactly was my burden for writing ministry? Using my then-immature concept of culture/literature, I explained my burden and how I had been moved. After a night of talking about this, it seemed he had a better sense of what I was saying. He broke into his well-known brilliant smile and pronounced his conclusion: "We may never see the vista you speak of before we die!"

It's true that the literature and culture ministry is not like a revival meeting, where one altar call can produce instantly visible, countable fruit. But this is the nature of callings — doing what God has called you to do and not questioning whether you are enough, whether you can do it, and whether there is fruit. This is faithfulness.

After many years of ministry, because for a long time I could not show any "products," and even after I had "products," not all of them were published in Christian publications the church circle was familiar with, the church still did not have a clear idea of what I was doing. They have never asked, so I have never offered a report. When the Chinese church circle in Los Angeles finally began to know me and I started conducting various seminars in churches, it had already been six years since I committed myself to the writing ministry. By that time, I was already frequently appearing in broadcast and magazine media.

One year, my husband attended a Chinese Christian media broadcasting seminar held in Los Angeles. When the seminar discussed the raising of people in media, the then general director of Kairos Communication Service International, Pastor Wei-Ran Zhao, suddenly mentioned me. He said that the Chinese church lacked a plan for cultivating talents; as an example, nobody knew how this "Mo Fei" had emerged. My husband laughed as he told me this after he came home.

For a long time, I was this baffling minister of the Kingdom. Not many people, including my own church, knew exactly what I was.

In God's kingdom, this rocky journey of growth is as Joseph from the Old Testament observed: "God meant it for good." God actually leads with His greater intent. In the Chinese church, literary and cultural mission is an area that needs to be developed. The various explorations in the dark were all a sort of "crying out in the wilderness," a preparation of the earth for the Kingdom's writing ministry.

This also caused me to especially have a burden for cultivating literature workers for the Kingdom, passing on the vision of the writing ministry, shepherding literature workers, and even perhaps helping them find a place in the church. For I have known firsthand how rocky and difficult it is for a literature worker.

Now, leading the Genesis Chinese Writing Ministry Institute, what I do the most is repeatedly defining for the Chinese church, "What is writing ministry? What is cultural mission?" This is based on my insights and experiences of more than 20 years of ministry.

Practicing Ministry, Building Legacy

It has been more than 20 years since I became a literature minister in 1988. In the beginning, my burden for the ministry was greater than my ability, so I asked God to give me ten years to equip myself. If, after ten years, my works find no place to be used and have never been published, I would promote the vision of a writing ministry by speaking, and encourage more competent Christian writers to participate in this form of ministry.

But after many years of practice in ministry, I gradually started to truly experience what Pastor Edwin Su had said from the beginning: God will keep developing the spiritual gifts, abilities, and skills one needs in order to carry out a more effective ministry for Him. My articles gradually were published, and book after book was released. I started to win literary awards one after the other, in quick succession and I could see that if I took a small step, God would encourage another. In this way, my ministry started to mature little by little.

When I published my first book in 1995, it was seven years after I had started trying. Since then, I have published more than ten books and received many literary awards both large and small. Perseverance was the key word. A lot of writers have more talent than I do, but they might quit after three or four years of trying. Maturity of any craft requires time. My publication and literary awards are all records highlighting how God elects someone and fosters this person into a writer for Him. Put another way, without God's appointing, this pen of Mo Fei would not exist.

By God's grace, after many twists and turns in writing, I finally carved out a small path. Looking back, this tortuous little path was necessary. The submissions and rejections and the experience of working out how to publish in non-Christian media have all now become part of what I can pass down.

When I entered my second decade of ministry, I felt that I had reached the phase where I could promote a vision. Coincidentally, in 2002, Ambassadors for Christ in Pennsylvania invited me to teach a class at their writing camp. At that time, Pastor Andrew Su (brother of Pastor Edwin) taught basic composition, interviewing and editing techniques, as well as the overall concept of the writing ministry. The writing class I taught alongside his was "Spiritual Formation and Advanced Creative Writing." Later on, Kingdom Resources for Christ took over hosting the Pennsylvania writing camp. Year after year, we developed a training plan together which grew more and more mature.

> We not only teach techniques and hone writing, we also pay more emphasis on spiritual character and servant attitude.

When I entered my third decade of ministry, after a lengthy period of discussion and prayer with Pastor Andrew Su, a co-worker of many years, we decided to found Genesis Chinese Writing Ministry Institute. In this institute, we hold to the tenet of "Workers before work, writers above writings, and sincerity before all else." We not only teach techniques and hone writing, we also pay more emphasis on spiritual character and servant attitude. We are spiritual mentors to our students, and whether in or out of the camp, we will continue to lead. This has become a kind of tradition; as Pastor Edwin Su originally called me and led me for a length of the path, now I pass it on in the same way.

Throughout the many years of our teaching experience, the writing, editing, translating, interviewing, and Internet ministries of the students have gradually blossomed and borne fruit. Besides individually writing articles and columns in traditional and electronic media, or publishing books, editing magazines, or receiving literary awards, they have gradually become a force to be reckoned with.

Looking back on the path I have walked these last twenty-some years, I can only say that blessed are those who can find their own life-altar. However, dedication to a calling is just like faith; seek and you will find, knock and the door will be opened. It all depends on whether you have the heart. So, do you have the heart? Is your pen being wielded for the Lord?

LEARNING TO WRITE

CATALINA REMBUYAN of Malaysia has had a checkered career as a writer, poet, performance artist and teacher. From the depths of rejection after rejection, she has also soared on the success of having her works published. But her journey is not yet done, and she continues to bring her feisty, creative energies to helping "enlighten the lives of others with knowledge of the finer, and more excellent minds that have gone before."

There are those who have found their vocation in a chosen field (dance, theatre, or whatever) who will probably claim that they've been dancing, singing or doing certain things before they could walk or talk. I never wrote before I could speak, but I have been telling stories for as long as I can remember. A kind of storytelling gene seems to run in my family; a gathering of extended relatives would involve relating and relaying anecdotes, liberally sprinkled with rhetorical devices of understatement or hyperbole — whichever aided the tale. My grandmother, a stoic woman who smoked, owned a gun, and raised three children on her own after her husband passed away, downplayed drama to tell better tales — chilling wintry cold was never colder than the mountains near home, places far away were never all too far. Her youngest son, my father, preferred hyperbole.

"I was at the airport when I encountered something I could not have imagined. I was not prepared for it. An emergency!"

("What emergency?" we'd ask, concerned.)

"The soles of my shoes came off!"

On another occasion when the loosening of soles from shoes was involved — this time on a shopping trip at a mall — my father started fretting and declaring that everyone, yes everyone around us, was staring!

(Only two people were.)

And so it seemed to be a kind of irony that when he saw that his daughter was telling stories, he became worried. I need to explain that, in her mind, she *was* telling stories, though it was really a haphazard way of talking to herself by assembling all the cartoon characters that she knew, imitating their manner of speech, and granting them new adventures that she set them on. These, she improvised for them willy nilly by means of spades, sticks, or any other pointed objects that could be wielded like magic wands to create landscapes and persons out of thin air.

The imagination of a child (even a child as old as 12, as I was) is a powerful thing; a kind of space between the world that is and the world that could be. I had the tendency to "see" ghosts, ghouls and monsters in the nooks and shadows of the house. When storms occurred in Kuching city (and Kuching, facing seawards, always had higher rainfall than Kuala Lumpur — where I've settled now) I would look upon the shapes of cumulonimbus clouds and it would seem to me that they, bearing death in the form of lightning strikes and bellowing their presence with thunder, also bore within them angry beings of black and grey — monsters that swirled in the sky. It probably did not help things too much that there was a spiritual revival going on in Sarawakian churches during that time, and while it led to much good (such as greater appreciation for theology and the Scriptures), one fairly unfortunate circumstance was a kind of awareness, or perhaps hyper-awareness, of the existence of demons.

> "Your daughter isn't strange," the counselor had said to my parents... She just needs a notebook."

Anyway, my parents started becoming paranoid about me becoming paranoid, and so they requested an appointment with a Christian child counselor. We had a brief conversation, during which I started wondering why we were even having a conversation in the first place (she asked me if I was naughty, and I felt rather talked down to and said I was not), but the session did yield some good.

"Your daughter isn't strange," the counselor had said to my parents, though I only found this out many years later. "She just needs a notebook."

I suppose if life were a story that would be its end; I would be armed with a notebook and would scribble down a masterpiece and win the world's hearts. No such thing happened, of course. My parents gave me a notebook, but the imagination that spurred my childhood years tumbled very awkwardly during my teenage years. I wrote as a young teenager, and then somehow and somewhere along the way, I grew older and I stopped.

For the first two years of secondary schooling, classes were held in the afternoon. We were part of what was conventionally called the 'afternoon session'; junior classes relegated to a different time frame for lessons in order to make the most of limited school premises. This turned out to be one of the greatest blessings of my teenage life. We, afternoon session students, would arrive early and, having nothing to do, we would wander about the school premises, talking among ourselves and sharing stories.

My school was an all-girls mission school built on Anglican church grounds that covered a great deal of hills and valleys, having been established during the reign of the Brookes.[1] Over the years that followed — from the reign of the Brooke monarchs to the Japanese Occupation, to the full inclusion of Sarawak in the British Empire, to the brief moment of national independence, and finally to being a part of Malaysia — the school maintained the green and natural environment of the hills. On the hills behind my school there were large trees, two or three of them possibly hundreds of years old, and in the afternoon the hills provided cool comfort and shade. There was also a kind of mystical and mysterious quality about these grounds. The hills (and the school itself) were once used as a camp for Japanese soldiers during the Occupation, and when I was eight or nine some of my classmates claimed that they had found a small tunnel in the hills, small enough for a child to climb into (the tunnel has since been sealed).

---

[1] British rulers of Sarawak from 1841–1946.

It was at this place that I shared stories with two of my other friends, Nasa and Pamela. Meeting at the hills to while our time away, we began first by sharing anecdotes about our lives (Nasa, like my father, had a gift of verbal storytelling) or talking about magazines or TV shows, and after we exhausted ourselves of anecdotes we started giving each other prompts that we would use to start writing novels. I completed my first novella under these circumstances: a story set in 17th century England during a time of highwaymen and misanthropes living in mansions on the moors (I'd read the Bronte sisters and was heavily influenced by them). It told the story of a young woman named Minerva whose life slowly unraveled when her rich Uncle Ebenezer was murdered by a scheming adventuress named Jezebel. Minerva is later rescued by a long-lost brother named Alan, a highwayman. The story had far too many murders simply because I didn't know what to do with the characters after I was done with them. Pamela wrote adventure stories, and Nasa, taking after horror novelists like Stephen King and her favourite TV series, *The X-Files*, wrote thrillers.

> I blame the Internet for both halting and helping my writing life. It introduced distractions.

This activity ended when we turned 15. At Form 3 we were shifted to the morning sessions and began cramming for our public examinations. Pamela and Nasa went into the Science stream, but I opted for the Arts. I did this because I wanted to study literature, but I also found myself rather lonely, and I spent more time forming friendships with people I found online. Around this time I started joining the Phases Young Writers' Mailing List.

I blame the Internet for both halting and helping my writing life. It introduced distractions. Most people claim that they started practicing writing by writing fanfiction. I was already comfortable with creating my own original characters and worlds, yet I regressed into fanfiction because I found that, unlike my original work, it gave me immediate gratification. I could post my story online and if it did well, I would earn praises for it. I was aware that this was shallow praise and that fanfiction had very little long-term worth, but I figured I could always do my original stuff later, and besides, I liked the socializing that I gained from being part of online fandoms. I certainly enjoyed the company of the people I met online more than the company of my classmates, whom I shared few interests with. I spent a lot of time chatting.

The Phases Young Writers' Mailing List probably redeemed a little of that lost time. The mailing list was a spin-off from *Phases* magazine, a youth magazine published by international Christian non-profit organization, Scripture Union. Initially I was not very much drawn to the *Phases* magazine as, well, the materials seemed a little too clever for my taste. Submissions from writers included entries into Top Ten Lists such as 'Top Ten Book Titles that Would Never Reach Bookstore Shelves.' There were also creative takes to prompts involving a story about *Hang Tuah* that was not about the Malay warrior but about the hanging of a man named *Tu Ah*. Then there was the subheading to two articles in the first issue I read: 'girl thinks she's a boy, boy thinks he's a clock, what is the world coming to?'

It turned out that the mailing list became my home away from home. There, I found my first introduction to science fiction and fantasy beyond Harry Potter; there, I was first introduced to theologians like C.S. Lewis; and there, I engaged in theological questions and discussions and was introduced to terms like "Calvinist" and "Arminian" for the very first time. It was an uncensored and unedited exchange of online interaction, full of flame wars, theological discussions, and quick creative writing. It was a world away from the world that I constantly found myself in: the faintly hypocritical rigidity that I found in church (church politics were rearing up following the charismatic revival in Sarawak, and there was a schism happening between the more charismatic-oriented Anglicans and the traditionalists), and the distressing depravity of the anecdotes related by my school friends: of going topless in laser disc centers, or of invitations to sex that turned into gang rapes that were in turn hushed up out of shame.

On the Phases Young Writers mailing list (or the Phyw, as we called ourselves), we fought, flamed, flirted, fell in love with one another, fell out of love with one another, and somehow — in the midst of all that mess — became pretty good friends. Of course, this is not to say that the Phyw was a bed full of roses that were bereft of thorns. For better or worse, this was also where I became acquainted with literary jealousy.

Publishing opportunities were rare in Malaysia in the Nineties, and jumping into this fray was an independent publisher called Silverfishbooks, the brainchild of a man named Raman. For several years, Raman would send out an annual call for submissions for an anthology called *Silverfish New Writing*. I sent my stories but they were never accepted. This blow was big enough for a young writer with a huge amount of faith in her self-worth (or, perhaps, merely a large ego), but the blow was worsened when other members of the Phyw sent in their submissions and were accepted. The hardest pill to swallow came from the first anthology, where a short story written by a boy much, much younger than me got through the slush pile. Zedeck (that is the name of the boy) had written a surreal story about sitting in a train on the LRT (Light Rapid Transit). I didn't like it as much as I liked mine; I thought my story was more deserving of attention, and when I found out that he had gotten through when I had been rejected, I went online and verbally abused him. In retrospect, I do not even remember the story that I had sent in, and I suspect it would be pretty terrible by my standards today, but I was jealous.

> **Learning to meet the tastes of the editors turned out to be an attempt to follow a moving goal post because the editors changed with every edition.**

Learning to meet the tastes of the editors turned out to be an attempt to follow a moving goal post because the editors changed with every edition. I remained jealous as more and more members of the Phyw had their work accepted into *Silverfish New Writing* (although no one has ever become the subject of verbal abuse since). A story that was written by a member whom I have always admired, Yoshua, about a soldier in Malaya was accepted in one anthology. Another story, called *Pringles*, was written by another Phywer named Yi-Jien Hwa in memory of his father who had passed away suddenly in an accident. Yi-Jien would later disappear while hiking, and his death and disappearance would shake and shape me in matters not immediately related to writing.

One day — I do not recall exactly when — I remember Yoshua saying to us: "So, do you think we can keep this tradition of having one story from a Phywer in each edition of *Silverfish New Writing*?"

The thing about the Phyw (that I regard now as being a very special thing, especially when I realize that most people in life have too little personal ambition rather than too much) was that by some strange alchemy, many of its members felt that they were brilliant. Not only did they know that they could write, they felt that they deserved recognition for writing. I suspect that this was largely due to the encouragement from our elders; we were often reminded that as members of the Phyw we were *few*, we were niche, we were quirky and, by extension, we were special. Perhaps it was self-indulgent, but it built confidence and raised standards. When Yoshua said this, he meant it both as an acknowledgment of the capabilities of the members of the Phyw and as a challenge for us.

I took it badly. The pride, the ambition, and the terrible rage from thwarted dreams and desires! I knew I could do it, I knew I deserved it, so why was I constantly shafted when other people got in? What magic formula did they have that I did not?

Anyway, bitter and resentful jealousy aside, I eventually moved to Kuala Lumpur and started getting involved in the editing and management of the *Phases* magazine itself. My first journalistic assignment with *Phases* was to search for people who did not buy pirated VCDs on principle, an assignment that I failed to fulfill. Many years later, I helped in organizing future Young Writers' Camps and shaping the direction of *Phases* magazine.

Sometimes, I was happy with the results that I got from my involvement with the team. We invited some very good speakers for some of our camps and I learned much from them. I was happy with how we were able to provide some experience for campers in interviewing, writing, and editing skills. Sometimes I was not that happy. Like all other print magazines, *Phases* hit on hard times. Recession was looming, funds were precious, and the pressure to move the entire publication online to cut costs was immense. We caved in to it. I gathered the experience from this misstep and turned it into lessons for learning. The demands and work processes of a magazine do not apply to an online publication, and I strongly believe that any attempt to move any print publication online without changing the work processes would be foolhardy.

> I knew I could do it, I knew I deserved it, so why was I constantly shafted when other people got in? What magic formula did they have that I did not?

Of course I did not move to Kuala Lumpur from Kuching just to be a part of the *Phases* magazine team. I studied Literature in English at the University of Malaya. I was an active student, participating in a number of club activities that included literary projects (a dramatic adaptation of Sophocles's *Oedipus Rex* and a very ambitious staging of *Romeo and Juliet* were among them), but I do not think I wrote very much, or very well. Oh yes, I blogged a lot and I continued writing fanfiction. That was not "real writing." "Real writing," to me, were the novels and novellas I had started dreaming up many years ago as a teenager and which have been suspended in hiatus: untouched, untapped and unwritten. Beyond fanfiction and blogging, the original writing I produced during this time was very poor. During this time I wrote mainly vignettes and short pieces that never extended beyond a few hundred-word drabbles.

See, I had fallen into this self-delusion that one could become a good writer through some form of osmosis from one's environment. I thought I could, like Prospero in the final act of *The Tempest*, create magic circles from mushrooms and shrubbery. If I read good writing (and I would always be doing that as an English major) I would become a good writer, right? (Well, I was wrong.) In the subsequent years I would come to realize that writers are workers before they are geniuses. During a creative writing workshop that I attended, the first thing I was told by the facilitator was that writers needed to treat their vocation with the same gravity that they treat their jobs. We were assigned to write about a thousand words each day, and were told that we could write anything and use any form of media as long as we were comfortable. We were encouraged to splurge. "Spend on a Moleskine if you have to," our facilitator advised us. I did not meet my daily targets, but the lessons I learned in that workshop I kept for life.

That workshop I attended was run by none other than Raman, organizer of the *Silverfish New Writing* series. This was the first of the creative writing workshops that would change the way I thought about writing; the second was the series of workshops on performing poetry organized by the British Council.

Several years ago the British Council in Malaysia brought performance poets from the United Kingdom to perform and conduct workshops in Kuala Lumpur. Among the ones who arrived in Malaysia to perform and teach were Francesca Beard, Jacob Sam-la Rose, Charlie Dark, and Malika Booker. During one of the workshops, Charlie Dark gave the second most crucial advice that I would ever receive as a writer: "Don't let petty jealousies and rivalries get to you. Remember that you're always stronger together than on your own."

This has been advice that has stuck. Too often, writers can get caught up in the illusion that they are competing against each other for acclaim, when the reality is that writers get better when they work together to draw attention and acclaim to themselves as a group. What is best for the community is best for the writer. By supporting each other instead of tearing each other down, writers create a community that is supportive and receptive of their creative material.

Charlie Dark's advice resonated in other workshop participants too. Kathleen, one of the workshop participants, started to organize get-togethers and meet-ups for the other participants. We eventually formed a collective and the name Poetry Underground was chosen. We met, practiced reading and performing, shared our poetry, and compiled our work. Two projects emerged from this collective: the first was an anthology called *Voices from the Underground*, and the second was a performance piece which we titled *Voices from the Underground II*.

> During a creative writing workshop that I attended, the first thing I was told by the facilitator was that writers needed to treat their vocation with the same gravity that they treat their jobs.

Unfortunately, if Charlie Dark's advice was the genesis of Poetry Underground, it was also the grounds for proving his advice true. In the later years of its formation one of the projects undertaken was to organize a series of poetry slams. There were problems at conception: could it be called a slam if the term is trademarked? Were Malaysian poets keen on competitive poetry? There were problems at implementation: meetings were organized but were not always attended, and tempers were beginning to rise over failure to meet obligations.

Then the deathblow was struck. Over e-mail exchanges, a member of the group asked a question on what the purpose of organizing literary events was. For another member, the question struck the wrong chord.

"I don't have time for these kinds of existential questions. People ask them everywhere and this is nothing new. We have to focus on getting things done. Action, that's what's important."

"These kinds of questions are important. It's the kind of questions we should ask ourselves about anything."

"Why do you always do this? You're always killing my drive to get anything done."

This is a brief account of what happened next: tempers flared, resentment was bared, foul words followed, and bridges were burned. By the end of the argument some people refused to work with one another, and for some this meant they were done with performing poetry. It seemed to me that the very thing Charlie Dark had warned us about had come true. We were breaking down. We'd allowed bitter fights among ourselves to get in the way of the art.

Of course the gradual ceasing of Poetry Underground's activities was not due to this flare up alone; some of our members changed jobs and had different commitments. Nor did the fracture lead to the death of grassroots-initiated literary events and activities as each member of the collective went on to initiate something else beyond Poetry Underground. I didn't stop writing poetry either, though my attentions were slowly shifting elsewhere, back to my old and first love: to stories.

Nanowrimo is an annual challenge to complete a novel of 50,000 words during the month of November. Participants would sign up on the official site, join forums to cheer and challenge each other, and those who could meet up in real time would do so on a weekly basis. I've signed up for Nanowrimo several times, but never really succeeded. I remember a vivid moment of attempt and failure: I was sitting in a dormitory room in college with a laptop before me. It was cold. I hammered the words of my Nanowrimo novel on to the white mock pages of Microsoft Word. I would stop, unhappy with my output. I never got beyond several hundred words.

One year — I can't exactly recall when, but it was after Raman's workshop, and a little after Kathleen left for Japan – I decided to attempt Nanowrimo again. I do not know why I thought I could do it that year, given the failures I had had so many years before. Perhaps it was because I had started reading Dostoevsky (*Crime and Punishment*, more specifically) and I realized that you could use a novel as a thesis for ideological exploration, with characters as mouthpieces for conflicting ideas. Perhaps I realized that, having started teaching in a private school, I would have a longer November break. Anyway, I made a very important decision that year: instead of typing my story out on Microsoft Word, I would write it down by hand.

Many, many years after attending Raman's workshop, I decided to finally take up his advice and splurged on my media. I bought a set of Moleskine cahiers. When I found out that my usual set of ballpoint pens created a dull, dreary and scribbly appearance on the paper, I bought a Pilot G-2 pen with a 1.0 nib. The black, wet ink would sink into the pages and form large blobs where lines crossed each other. To me their dark forms looked aesthetically pleasing. They made the drafts worth looking at. They were beautiful.

That year, I completed my draft of a 50,000-word novel for Nanowrimo and won. The story was not all that great: a Singaporean boy falls into a coma and is spirited away into a fantasy land where he must become a hero (a story not unlike thousands of other fantasy works out there), but the habit I picked up while writing it stuck with me. Sometimes, getting writing done is simply a matter of finding the right rituals: Virginia Woolf needed a room of her own, the frequent settings of isolated cabins in Stephen King novels suggest authorial familiarity with such locations, and Ernest Hemingway observed others from cafes. I use single-lined paperback notebooks (there are good Moleskine knock-offs out there) and I handwrite all my drafts with a black Pilot G-2 pen.

I'd like to end this little narrative with some points of triumph — the kind of happy notes of writers gaining showers of accolades and achievements after a long period of toil and rejection — but the truth is, writing is very often a process where one goes through lots of ups and downs.

My writing ritual paid off. I've written several stories ever since I ditched drafting on Microsoft Word and opted for Moleskines (or knock-offs), along with writing by hand. I had some of them published by a friend of mine, TshiungHan See, who runs a zine called *New Village*.

I have not abandoned poetry. Last year, I decided that after the many years of being involved in performance poetry, I was finally ready to compile my first chapbook. Called *Spokes*, I sold it at a local arts market called Art for Grabs and through Silverfishbooks. It didn't exactly fly off the shelves and I was initially disappointed by how low sales were, but I covered all my costs and I took some pleasure from knowing that, despite having no name for myself, a number of people out there thought that my work was worth paying for. This year, three of my poems have been published in an anthology compiled by Professor Ghulam Sarwar-Yousof (an academic expert on Asian traditional theatre and poetry), called the *Asian Centre Anthology of Malaysian Poetry in English*.

But I continue to know rejection. Somehow, after many years of failure and learning from them, I thought I had finally hit on the formula of what worked for me as a writer. I wrote a story and took many days editing and re-writing it. When I found out it was not accepted for publication in an anthology, I was crushed. At that time, I had hit a rough point in my personal life (I'd failed at love, again) and I was overwhelmed by the constant streaming of Malaysia Airlines MH370 news on every single media outlet I encountered. I gave in to temptation, bought a pack of Marlboros, and smoked at Starbucks until midnight.

The nights of self-doubt and existential questions about the greater picture are still there. The lack of sleep from three-hour nights happens more often. There is a sense of awareness that success and fame are fleeting and that it is vital, as with all other human endeavors, to anchor it to the source of all that is noble, pure, lovely, praiseworthy and true (to quote St. Paul's letter to the Philippians), but to also have that drive buffeted by questioning and doubt.

> I wrote a story and took many days editing and re-writing it. When I found out it was not accepted for publication in an anthology, I was crushed.

I suppose I do have a good ending for this essay.

A story of mine has been accepted for a short-story anthology. Called 'The Kill Wish,' the story appears in *KL Noir: Yellow*, an anthology of crime-oriented tales set in Kuala Lumpur. The publisher revealed that there were a hundred submissions (I had submitted two) so I had no idea how likely I was to have my story accepted. It seemed that after all these years, and after such a very long time of unlearning bad habits and learning new ones, I had finally learned to write.

I am still learning how to write. I am writing still, and with each new project I am learning.

The years that I had dedicated to writing for *Phases* has helped me in another area of my life that I had not always associated with writing: my life as a teacher. I am currently teaching the A-Levels at a local college and part of my job involves overseeing the students' campus magazine, *The A-Voice*. The experience that I had picked up with *Phases* has allowed me to manage young writers — all of them at the exact age I was when I was involved in *Phases* — and I feel a sense of fulfillment in knowing that by guiding them I am helping them gain greater experience for work and life.

I continue to write and perform poetry. I've gained greater confidence on stage and a stronger sense of my performing and writing style as a poet. I haven't seen any significant ways that my involvement in poetry has blessed or enriched others, but I am beginning to see how my faith is informing my poems.

I have learned to handle rejection. After 'The Kill Wish' was accepted into *KL Noir: Yellow*, I received no less than three rejections for my other stories submitted to other publishers. Unlike my previous experience of rejection when I ended up wallowing in coffee and cigarettes, I brushed aside these setbacks and moved on.

I have discovered — or at least am discovering — that with every act of writing and engagement in the field of literature I see (or perhaps, to the skeptics out there, I imagine) God's hand in my life. Perhaps my calling is not to be a brilliant writer but a hardworking one. Perhaps my duty is not to be the shining star in a sky full of bright bards but to enlighten the lives of others with knowledge of the finer, and more excellent minds that have gone before: not only the Keatses, Shakespeares and Lessings but also those who have made Christ their Muse — the Donnes, the Miltons, the Manley-Hopkinses, the Tolkiens, and many, many others.

I have no idea if I will finish well, or if any of what I do will amount to any good in the end, but I don't intend to stop.

OUT OF THE KILLING FIELDS

Too often one reads about the horrors and atrocities that occurred during the Cambodian Civil War. But not often enough does one read of how God's guiding hand shines through such trials and tribulations and carries one into the safety of knowing Him.

SEILA UON's journey shows how God reveals Himself in our lives in the most unexpected of times and in ways that we least expect — through a simple piece of paper found in a basket. He tells us of how God was with him all through the war up to the time when he first begins to write. Today, Seila uses his gift of words to continue to impact those around him as executive director of DOVE Ministries which is involved in the training of emerging church leaders.

The Killing Fields of Cambodia in the 1970s were not the place or time to learn how to write. Nor were the following years, when Vietnam expelled the Khmer Rouge communists and occupied the country. Vietnam began to recruit young men like me to join their army. They placed Cambodian soldiers at the front so we would step on the landmines, get blown up, and make the road safe for the Vietnamese soldiers. That's when I escaped to a refugee camp in Thailand, where I stayed for 12 years.

All during this time I was not writing. You could say I was collecting experiences of horror and pain for the day when I would write. I knew nothing in those days about a God who cared for me and who might have a plan for me. It wasn't until much later that I realized He was with me all the way. This should be an encouragement to others who may spend months, even years, before they write.

Late in January 1971, at about 2:30 pm, I watched as a small plane flew over our village in eastern Cambodia. The plane banked away and shot a puff of smoke in the sky. A few minutes later, two giant American planes, looking like silver arrowheads, roared over and dropped bombs on our village. They were cluster bombs and the small pieces cut into houses and people, and everything was on fire.

This was my first memory of war — when America was fighting the Viet Cong. After that day, I hated Americans for 20 years, but I didn't write anything that whole time.

I grew up with buffalos and cows. I was so happy on the farm. But after the bombs, my family became displaced persons in Phnom Penh. My father couldn't afford to send me to school. Most of us poor boys stayed with the monks at the pagoda, where we would be fed. This was only in the mornings, though. In the evenings, we had to look for food in the town. One night I said to one of my pagoda friends, "I have an idea."

"What?"

"Let's get bread and sell it for money to buy food."

We got up at four the next morning, picked up bread from the bakery, and sold it in the street. It didn't teach me how to write, but I was able to earn some money to buy food. Some days, I couldn't sell any bread, and so I just kept it and ate it for dinner. By then the bread that was crispy and warm and fresh in the morning was cold and tough.

I lived that way for four years while the Khmer Rouge were fighting our government to take over the country. All during this time, I sold bread. In fact, when the bombs were dropping all around us, we could sell even more bread because people were afraid. Many lived on the third floor of their buildings, and they would not come down to the street. They dropped a line of string down to me, weighted with a battery and some money. I put the bread in place of the money and they pulled the string up with the bread.

> **We were worried about becoming soldiers. We knew that if we signed up, we would be killed quickly — forced to walk over the landmines in front of the Vietnamese soldiers.**

So for me, whenever the shelling started, my business was good. Life was good.

The Khmer Rouge took over Phnom Penh in 1975, and everyone was evacuated into the provinces to become slaves in the rice fields. Millions died of starvation, or they were murdered by Khmer Rouge soldiers. I was sent back to my village where for two years I went up into the mountain and smashed rocks to make gravel.

When Vietnam started a war with Cambodia in 1978, the war spilled over to my village, and I had to escape once more. It was a terrifying time. The Khmer Rouge were spreading rumors that when the Vietnamese arrived in a place, they would kill everyone. Cambodians scurried all around, their eyes wide with fright. To get to Phnom Penh, we had to cross the Mekong River, but only Khmer Rouge soldiers were allowed on the ferries. So people would try to swim across the river, but the current was strong, and they drowned.

I asked my mother if I should try to swim across, but she said, "Don't swim — it's better to die all together on the ground than to drown by yourself in the river."

We had to flee back to my village, which was over 90 kilometers away. I slept along the road next to my brother and sister. One day, my brother became dehydrated and died. When we reached our village, we found only an empty house. All our livestock was gone — stolen by the Khmer Rouge or refugees escaping along the road by our house.

We tried to farm again. But we had no ox for the plough. We started helping the neighbors with their water buffalo. The neighbors, in turn, helped us plough our field. We planted two hectares of rice. We had a good crop, but then the flood came and destroyed our house and all the rice. That left us starving. We worked for others to get food. The next year, we planted again, but this time drought killed everything.

Men from our Vietnamese-supported government came to our village. They said, "We need soldiers to fight in the guerilla war against the remaining Khmer Rouge fighters on the border with Thailand."

We only had six young men in our village — all the rest were widows from the killing fields. What to do? We were worried about becoming soldiers. We knew that if we signed up, we would be killed quickly — forced to walk over the landmines in front of the Vietnamese soldiers. They decided to hold a lottery. They would put our names in a hat, and the name that was picked would have to go. I discussed the situation with my Mom and Auntie. (The rest of my family had died.) They agreed, "You have to flee."

But how to escape? I had no money. There was no money anywhere in the whole country. To get something, you had to barter. My Auntie had a bicycle with no tubes or rubber tires, only the metal rims. My Mom gave me 15 scoops of rice.

I started off for Thailand with 15 scoops of rice, riding on the metal rims of Auntie's bicycle. The trucks that passed me were all filled with Vietnamese soldiers, and they demanded some form of payment before they would give me a ride. Once I caught a hen, and I gave it to a truck driver who gave me a ride.

Another time, I sat with my bicycle next to me on the back of a horse cart — for three scoops of rice. Finally, I arrived in Phnom Penh and rode my bike to the railroad station, where I slept all night on the platform.

> ## I wrote nothing during those days, but it was through writing that I became a Christian.

Early in the morning, a train came that was going west, but the carriages were full of ammunition and rice — the passengers were all sitting on the roof. I tried to find a place on the roof but there was no room. One man directed me to a carriage in front of the locomotive. It was filled with sandbags and wood, but I dragged my bicycle up on the roof where I sat the whole way. I didn't find out until we reached Battambang that the carriage I was sitting on was put there to blow up landmines on the tracks — and protect the locomotive. Still, I made it without being killed. Many hundreds were killed on trains during that time — mostly women and children as the men had all been killed earlier.

Before I reached the Thai border, I sold my bicycle. With the money, I hired an oxcart, a simple wooden cart attached to two oxen. We had one driver, plus an uncle and his cousin, and myself. We crossed the border safely, and my life in a refugee camp began.

In the United Nations (UN) camp, only women and children were allowed to get food. So, many of the men would find a woman and marry her, just to eat. Or they would dress up like women to get food. Even though I still was not a Christian, I thought this was wrong, so I refused. Instead, I started a new business — selling ice.

I bought a large block of ice from the Thai and then smashed it into pieces and sold the pieces in little sacks. That was how I survived; at least until the monsoon rains, when people stopped buying ice. Each day, all my ice would melt, and I would lose money.

I decided to buy eels and sell them in the camp. One day, I spent my money on an eel and brought it in a basket to camp at night to sell the next morning. During the night, it rained so hard, my basket filled up with water, and the eel escaped. After that, I bought and sold chickens.

I wrote nothing during those days, but it was through writing that I became a Christian. That's why I am so committed to writing and to training writers today.

Here is how it happened. I decided to sign up to be trained as a nurse. My first job as a nurse was to provide vaccinations to children, working with an organization called Youth with a Mission (YWAM). I had to weigh the children in a basket, measure their height, and write details on a yellow nutrition card.

YWAM had to follow the UN rule not to proselytize, but they were clever and would sneak Christian tracts into the baskets where we weighed the children. One day, I read one of the tracts, written by a Russian philosopher.

The Russian philosopher told the story of a man walking in a forest who saw a tiger and ran from it in fear. The man tumbled over a cliff, but grabbed hold of a vine, which kept him from falling to the river below into the jaws of a crocodile. The man looked up... and saw the tiger. He looked down... and saw the crocodile. He looked up again, and he saw a mouse starting to gnaw on the vine.

This is what life is like without Jesus Christ, explained the Russian philosopher. Whether we climb up or down, we will die, and if we do nothing, we will die because soon the mouse will chew through the vine.

After reading this story, I started asking what it meant to be a Christian. I met with an Australian on the YWAM staff who took the time to answer my questions. A year later, I was baptized.

After four or five years with YWAM, in 1989, I joined the evangelistic team of Campus Crusade for Christ, and we traveled to different parts of the camp. Two years after that, I was repatriated back to Cambodia and continued to work with Campus Crusade for Christ. With YWAM, my salary had been two bags of rice and 12 cans of fish. Campus Crusade started paying me $20, but then this ended after two years.

> I learned that writing had to do not only with words and memories, but structure and planning.

I had learned English with YWAM, and so I got a job with the Jesuits teaching English for $40. Oh, life was so good. I had become rich with $40 to spend!

I should mention here that when I was in Thailand, I met and married my wife. I had hated Americans up till then, but my wife's Aunt was in the USA, and from that moment on I loved Americans and wanted to go to the United States. But God had a different plan. He wanted me to return to Cambodia to help my people, and I know he allowed me to suffer and live in a camp for a purpose. I have met Cambodians in America, and they are rich, but they are so busy making money, they have no time for other people nor for their children. I am so much happier working for my own people in my own country.

During the next four years, the UN Transitional Authority organized the first election in Cambodia. Though I was not writing — working again for YWAM — I was interested in writing so I accepted an invitation to attend a writing workshop in Phnom Penh led by Larry Brook from the David C. Cook Foundation in America. (I helped interpret too.)

At this workshop I learned that writing had to do not only with words and memories, but structure and planning. Larry taught us different "writing maps" that we could follow so we would know where to begin and where to end and not get lost. When we wrote a meditation, we could follow the meditation map. The article map was for writing articles. The short story map was for writing fiction or a folktale. The maps were flexible enough to put in our own culture and language.

We learned to draw a cartoon of our writing first so that our writing would have plenty of action and concrete details, and not just abstract ideas.

Not long after that, God led me to work for World Vision, where I began my work in translation and writing, especially for a new magazine called *Honeycomb*. *Honeycomb* was where I could put Larry's writing maps to good use. I had to write articles and allegories every three months. I also had to go out and interview people. When I couldn't find someone to interview, I had to write an article based on my own ideas and experiences. I could look back to my life in my village, to the bombs falling and the killing fields, to my life as a refugee in Thailand.

While I wrote, I never really thought about our readers, until they began writing to me and saying, "I really liked that article." Or "That article really helped me in my Christian life."

I have kept on writing ever since, even after I left World Vision and joined DOVE (Develop Our Village Economy). This is a village development agency to build youth and leaders in the provinces. I wrote more articles and even collaborated with missionary Brian Maher on *Cry of the Gecko*, which is a history of the church in Cambodia. But then, working again with Larry, in a series of workshops over a three-year period sponsored by Fount of Wisdom, a Christian publisher in Phnom Penh, I wrote my own first book, *Love and Marriage*, which was published this past year.

A few months ago, I was visiting Battambang when two pastors came up to me and said they had enjoyed reading my articles in *Honeycomb*. One of them said, "I have been so blessed by your writing… why don't you write again?"

I assured them that I had. I told them about *Love and Marriage* and other books by my friends Nara and Savy, amongst others, and promised to bring copies to sell at a good price on my next visit.

It's an exciting time now in Cambodia for Christian writers. More are writing and publishing than ever before. Just this week we launched a new writers' group that will seek to encourage and train even more writers.

There is more to tell — about the past, the present, and our hopes for the future. But I'll stop here because my purpose has been simply to write a brief account of one Cambodian man's journey from years of war, suffering and survival… to writing.

A FISHBONE IN MY THROAT

ANDREW YUAN is a marriage family counselling expert and a famous speaker and author. Yuan has researched on marriage, family and parenting issues since the 1990s, and has been awarded the title, "China's Family Warden". He has trained with the American Family Association and is a certified international speaker.

In the *Must-Read for Parents* ("父母必读") magazine, Yuan started a column on parenting called "Heartfelt Exchanges". The success of this column has enabled him to speak about marriages and families in over 20 provinces in China. Yuan's lively seminars, based on the Bible and combined with 16 years of counselling experience and case studies, have been well received by pastoral staff and loved by the audiences.

Yuan's "Strengthening the Marital Vow" marriage and family ministry also conducts training on Christian love, avoiding marital mistakes, parenting, etc.

I started my marriage ministry in 1999. As a result of this ministry, I have published a total of four books and two DVDs.

How Did I Begin on This Journey of Writing?

I was a university teacher and had taught in the Beijing Foreign Studies University (the current College of Foreign Studies of Capital Normal University) and the Foreign Trade University. When I went to Korea in 1993, I chanced upon and, for the first time, walked into a Korean church and was awestruck by the hymns of praise. Although I had always regarded myself as a very good man, I could not help but feel very filthy and unworthy to stand in the holy church. Hence, when the pastor asked if anyone would like to receive Jesus, I expressed the willingness to accept Jesus even though I could not fully understand the sermon. It was only after that that I received the truth more systematically in an international church. My wife, who had received the Lord earlier than I, joined me in Seoul later and we served together in a church.

Strengthening Family Ties in China

Due to the long separation from my son, who was then already nine, I missed him dearly and longed to see him. I thought then that when I saw my son, regardless of how tall he was, I would hug him tightly for as long as I wished, for I had missed him so much. However, when I actually saw him and rushed over to hug him, not only did he not respond, he pushed me away a few times. I was very heartbroken. I kept asking God, *"Why doesn't the son that I miss so dearly have any affection for me?"* Then God told me, *"Don't you see? Though you have now gotten some of the things you longed for, you have lost the more precious things that I had in store for you."* My wife and I decided not to separate the family again. Later, when God showed me clearly that He wanted me to go back to China to serve Him, we went back without hesitation.

The Happy Reunion

After returning to China, I took the posts of vice-principal and director of the international department in a private school. Understanding the importance of the family unit, I brought my wife and son to the school where I was serving. I did not want the family to be separated again. What touched me was my wife's self-sacrifice and commitment to the family. It was then that my wife, withstanding pressure from various sources, resigned from her job, and returned home to be a full-time mother; to keep her husband and child company every day. Although our income was reduced and the living standard greatly lowered, being a family that could interact with each other every day became the envy of many students and colleagues. I was working at a "school for aristocrats" whose students were all from "successful" families with parents who were high officials, wealthy, and powerful people whom others aspired to be. However, surprisingly, most of the students' original families were broken. It was then that I clearly heard God asking me whether I would want to be one of these successful people. My response was very clear, "*If this is the price of success, I do not want it!*" I had already come to understand that no success could compensate for a failed marriage and a broken family.

> The key place of educational development is in the family, not the school. Children show forth in school the influence they had received from their families.

In 1996, I represented the school at an international academic conference for high school principals in the United States. That learning experience caused me to understand more deeply the important influence of the family on the emotions and personality of a child. The key place of educational development is in the family, not the school. Children show forth in school the influence they had received from their families. This new perspective completely overturned my previous educational philosophy.

Returning home, I used the information on family and parenting I had brought back from the United States to open up a channel of communication with parents and started offering them an article on parenting once a month. As such messages were hard to come by in China, they were very well received. At the same time, this greatly inspired my interest in writing and my enthusiasm in the research on marital and family problems. I think, even then, God was already preparing me for the ministry in this area.

Receiving God's Calling and Training in Marital and Family Matters

In 1998, I joined an American training company in the Mainland as a trainer. As all the foreign employees were Christians, I was able to interact with traditional Christian families that followed biblical principles in their work and family life. I was touched when I saw how harmonious and happy their husbands and wives were, and how orderly and obedient their children were.

In the spring of 1999, with the support of the company, my wife and I attended "Family Life," an American international training program held in Canada for speakers. During the graduation ceremony, I clearly heard God's calling for me, *"This is what I want you to do in China."* I told my mentor what God had told me and, during the closing ceremony, all the speakers from various countries laid hands on and prayed for us that God would walk with us.

The First Marriage Ministry

I had once shared the Gospel with a foreign couple working in Beijing and helped them receive Christ. They wanted to be married but did not have the money to hold a wedding. Upon returning home from the United States, my wife and I decided to hold a wedding for them at our home and to use this wedding to give my first message on biblical marriage. The attendees of the wedding were brothers and sisters in Christ and so the response to the message was very good. From then on, I began to receive more invitations to give lectures. After a couple of years, although I was more familiar with the content of my lectures and more confident of my delivery technique, the responses from our brothers and sisters were very far from our own. I had thought that basing my programs on the Bible would be sufficient. It was then that I realized that what our brothers and sisters wanted to see was how the instructor lived out these principles practically in his own life. I started to focus more on the practice of these principles in my own marriage and family. I also observed the state of Christian marriages in China at that time. Gradually, I departed from the original textbook and wrote new content of the programs based on the local context. During that same period, I was also publishing a monthly article on parenting in a column I started called "Confluence of the Rivers of Hearts" in the biggest parenting magazine, *A Must Read for Parents*. Although these articles could not speak directly on the Christian faith and, looking back, lacked spiritual depth, they did receive good commendations. This could be said to be the start of my writing career.

Initially, my marriage counseling programs catered not only to those in the faith but also to other societal groups. Naturally, the speaking invitations from these societal groups carried the condition that I was not to touch openly on the Christian faith. Once, after teaching a course on parenting to a big corporation, although the audience responded positively, there was not any joy in my heart. I asked God quietly why that was so.

God asked me, "*What are you doing?*"

I said, "*I am speaking to these non-believers about marriage and parenting. I want to save them!*"

God asked me, "*Can you save them without mentioning My name?*"

This question was a shock to me. Indeed, how can anyone be saved if the name of Christ is not mentioned? I replied immediately, "*Of course not. But at least, I can improve the quality of their lives.*" God said, "*By simply improving the quality of their lives without the cross, aren't you watching them go happily toward hell?*" I was dumbfounded. It is true — if our problems can be solved without the cross, Jesus would not be the way, the truth, and the life. "What am I to do?" God told me, "I want you to focus on issues in the families of God. There are many broken Christian families. Only when the families of the children of God are strengthened and established, can those who reject me be truly influenced." From then on, my service started to have three "focuses":

- ♦ Focusing the content on the Bible (the analysis of God's law);
- ♦ Focusing on the church (God's family) as the target of my service; and
- ♦ Solving problems by focusing on the work of the Holy Spirit (to bring about changes in the life of the target persons).

During the early stage of the ministry, after a talk I gave to a church in Chengdu, Peng Qiang, a brother whose ministry was the publishing of Christian books, proposed to help me publish the very first Christian book written by a Chinese on the subject of marriage and family. Using the material and the recording of my talk, they very quickly finished the original draft of the book which they passed to me for the final review. However, I procrastinated editing the draft after receiving it. That was because I was not very sure of the quality of my talk. I felt that my marriage was still undergoing tests and much of the content of my talk was what I had learnt from others. It was not sufficiently mature yet to be published into a book. However, I was too embarrassed to explain to Peng Qiang and his team, for they had regarded the project as a great and important one and had finished the work with great drive and speed. How could I simply quit? But I continued to procrastinate. Soon after, I heard that brother Peng Qiang had gone to the United States to study and the matter came to a natural rest. (The project was delayed for a few years, during which time I always felt very apologetic to Peng Qiang and his team. It was only a few years later when I met Peng Qiang again in Beijing, after his return from the United States, that I apologized to him, pleaded for his understanding, and compensated them somewhat for their losses.) Nevertheless, I knew that even if the book were to be published, it would not have withstood the test, as the programs still contained too many methods and techniques, and the content of the book lacked life since my life was still in the process of maturing.

> ... my own marriage was facing a great trial at that time. I even doubted the content that I taught in my own marriage programs.

In 2006, I received an invitation from the McDowell Ministry Team to record two DVDs: *Six Important Factors for Building up Children* and *True Love — Follow Me*. Although there were many obstacles during the process of the recording, the programs received very good feedback and many accepted the Christian faith after watching the DVDs. A doctoral student's supervisor from a university in Yunnan bought 60 copies for his colleagues and relatives, and the student herself accepted Christ too. She even came personally to Beijing to express her gratitude. This, to me, was a great encouragement.

It was then that I had the urge to write, for I saw that only in books could I fully express what I wanted to say. I prayed to God and asked whether I should stop giving talks and focus on writing. God's answer was for me to continue to focus on perfecting the programs. For only through such work would my programs become fuller and their effect more lasting. God also told me that when it is time to write and publish, He would send someone to help me.

True enough, in 2007, an organization started me off on writing a book on marriage. The political environment at that time was more open than in the past and there were fewer restrictions on the publication of religious books. After much consideration, I decided to use the contents of my pre-marriage counseling program as the first book. This was a book on preparing for marriage. I could finally openly use the actual biblical scriptures in this book. Thanks to the prevailing political climate, it was easier to publish books on pre-marital relationships. Even then, it took two years from the completion of the writing of the book to its publication, and not until after many rounds of censorship reviews. It was only in 2009 that the approval for the publication was given. That was the birth of *How to Find the Right Other-Half.*

Another reason for writing a book on pre-marital relationships and not on marriage itself was that my own marriage was facing a great trial at that time. I even doubted the content that I taught in my own marriage programs. Hence, I decided to leave it alone for a while.

Earlier in 1994, when my wife and I were overseas, my wife had thyroiditis. The thyroid is an important organ. When we are tired, shocked, angry, or excited, it works as a buffer and plays a balancing role. The illness damaged my wife's thyroid and the level of its secretion was down to zero. We were overseas and had no money to treat her illness and we did not have insurance. We had just accepted Christ and, during our hardship, Zhou Suqin, the wife of Pastor Zhou Guangliang of Good Friend Program Station, helped us by giving us free treatment.

Due to her illness, my wife would get tired and have frequent mood swings. As I was in the marriage ministry, I did my best to bear with her strange temperament. At the same time, I was "proud" that I could do so.

When my wife reached menopause in her fifties, her condition worsened. She experienced severe mental depression and deteriorated to the stage where she did not want to be in contact with anyone. She did not want to talk nor do anything. She was cold to everyone and even our relatives found her unapproachable. I went out to preach but came back to a home that was in a mess. Although I grumbled and was not happy, no matter how late I came home, I would immediately roll up my sleeves and do the chores. I had to teach and also bear the burden of buying the groceries, cooking, cleaning the house, and other household chores. There was a long period of time when she would lie on the bed the whole day long. If this had gone on, her muscles would gradually atrophy. Therefore, I had to make great efforts daily to get her out of the bed to walk around. After a while, she could not even walk and I had to massage the muscles of her limbs daily. No matter how much I did, her condition did not improve in any significant way. Under such a situation, my heart was extremely miserable and the feeling of any happiness was completely gone. Since I was in the marriage ministry and had a certain level of reputation in church, I had to endure even when it was difficult to do so. I had to disguise my pain in front of others and felt that I was being held hostage by the "happiness" that I preached.

I prayed, "*Oh God, I am doing exactly what I preach. Why isn't there any good result? If all these cannot solve my own problems, how can they solve the problems of my audience? How can I build happiness in others, when I myself am not happy?*" I was so grieved that I even thought about death. Once, I knelt down and banged my head continually against the floor, crying profusely. After the prayer, there was a big bruise on my head. When I visited my mother, she asked me what had happened to my head. I even had to lie and told her that I had accidentally banged my head on the door frame. She asked, "Where did you find such a low door frame?" During my daily prayer then, I questioned God constantly, "*Why is it that I, a builder of family happiness, do not have happiness in my own family? Where have I erred? Why, after doing so much, am I less happy that those who do not even try? What more should I do if I still cannot be happy after trying so hard? Do you*

> I had to disguise my pain in front of others and felt that I was being held hostage by the "happiness" that I preached.

want to make things more difficult when many people are feeling that what I am preaching now is already difficult to attain?"

When I was questioning God one day, He suddenly said to me, *"My marriage was not a happy one too."* I was shocked and thought that I had heard wrongly. God told me, *"If marriage is meant to be happy, I would have given you a model marriage in the Bible. However, you saw my marriage filled with conflicts from the very beginning. My wife (the Israelites) betrayed me time and again, and in the end, even nailed me to the cross. Although there wasn't any happiness, I loved her nonetheless, because this was the pledge that I had given to her!"*

I was instantly enlightened. My heart received the comfort that I never had before and tears immediately poured out of my eyes.

I asked Him again, *"Oh God, my wife doesn't talk to me. How can I communicate with her and let her know what I feel?"*

God said, *"We have piped unto you, and ye have not danced; we have mourned unto you, and ye have not lamented. (Matthew 11:17) There is no better communication than mine, but my wife (the Israelites) did not understand too and did not listen at all."*

"Oh God, why must I have such a painful experience?"

"To let you understand that marriage does not mean happiness."

"Then what does marriage entail?"

"It entails unconditional self-commitment."

God said, *"I treated my wife infinite times better than you have treated yours, but my wife still did not obey nor understand me, and our relationship was filled with conflicts and quarrels. Despite all this, I continued to commit myself to my promise to her. You also promised her before your wedding that in sickness and in health, for richer or for poorer, you will love her forever. This is the time to test whether you will be committed to the promise that you had made."*

In that moment, my heart was filled with the Holy Spirit.

The second book, *Hand in Hand through the River of Life*, was completed during this period of pain. This book was compiled from the transcripts of the audio and video recordings of my talks over several years. The burden of taking care of my wife was very heavy then and it was difficult for me to have the energy to complete the writing of the book alone. God sent His angels to help me. Two sisters used their precious time to help me with editing and layout. The book was finally completed in 2010. What excited me more was that the two sisters' views on marriage were greatly changed in the process. Their relationships with their husbands were greatly improved. This increased my confidence in the impact of this book.

> That the two sisters' views on marriage were greatly changed in the process. Their relationships with their husbands were greatly improved.

I want to thank God specially for giving my wife and me our painful marriage to try us, which caused me to break away from the scripted-style marriage programs, to find my own way. This book is different from the majority of marriage programs in that it does not focus on solving problems in marriage, such as improving communication, easing conflicts, teaching romantic techniques, and how to open a "love bank" or "love account" in each other's heart, but rather on seeking God's will and principles in the Bible. The censorship review of this book took less than a year and it was officially published in 2011.

Before this, another Christian publisher had voiced an interest in a DVD that I had recorded specially to explain the spiritual meaning of marriage. They wanted this to sell well, so they designed a "dazzling" packaging for it. The shine of this disc was the light that the

Holy Spirit gave me during my most trying period. It contributed greatly to the increase of my faith even in the midst of my pain.

I wish to make special mention of the book that was recently published — *Walking Out of the Wrong Zone in Marriage*. This book was based on my 15 years of understanding the essence of marriage and was also the most challenging book for me.

I thought that once I could commit myself fully to my marriage, God would deliver my wife from her infirmities. Little did I know that my wife's condition would continue to be unstable and without any fundamental change. One day, in my prayer, God asked me, "*If your wife continues to be in this condition, will you still love her?*" I hesitated for a while and said, "*Of course!*" God asked again, "*If I do not heal your wife, will you still love Me?*" My eyes filled with tears, but I said, "*Yes.*" God said to me, "*Accept the pain that your wife's illness will bring you. My grace is sufficient for you!*" It was then that I deeply understood that this was the thorn that God had put in my flesh and it was this thorn that had caused me to understand the meaning of marriage. In my life, God had made all things work together for good, to the benefit of man. This is especially true in marriage. The trials I had to go through subverted my past understanding of marriage: that man and woman should have gender equality, that marriage is a means of companionship, and that the objectives of marriage are happiness and harmony. I was very reluctant to complete *Walking Out of the Error Zone in Marriage* because this book records the fundamental change in my understanding and attitude on marriage after walking through "the valley of the shadow of death." In it are my heartfelt words to my readers and audience. I know that this book will surely bring about many doubts and even attacks, but the Holy Spirit within me convicted me to share what I had learnt. *For woe is unto me, if I preach not this.*

Writing is like having a fishbone in your throat. You have to get it out.

GRACEW♥RKS

Graceworks is a publishing and training consultancy based in Singapore, dedicated to promoting spiritual friendship in church and society, and seeing lives transformed through books that present truth for life.

Our publications can be found on our online store, *www.graceworks.com.sg*. Paperbacks are also available on Bookdepository and Amazon and eBooks on Kindle, iBooks and Kobo.

You can contact us at *enquiries@gracework.com.sg,* or follow us on Facebook (@GraceworksSG) and Instagram (graceworkssg).

The power of the written word to transform lives and nourish believers shines in the world's difficult places. The potential impact is huge where readers are most hungry for hope and encouragement. To combat the lack of homegrown literature that will speak to hearts, minds and daily needs, MAI equips men and women to create life-changing books and articles in their own heart languages.

Since our founding in 1985, MAI has led 430 training programs in 85 countries on 5 continents with 9,500 people equipped. We have seen budding writers developed, publishing houses grown, periodicals launched and books produced. We celebrate as God strengthens the Church and draws hungry readers to Christ with the written word.

You can learn more at *https://littworld.org/.*

www.ingramcontent.com/pod-product-compliance
Lightning Source LLC
Chambersburg PA
CBHW030248130626
46549CB00002B/447